KATY BESKOW

VEGAN PANTRY

10 Staple Ingredients, 100 Plant-Based Recipes

Photography by Luke Albert

quadrille

INTRODUCTION

What ingredients do you always have in your pantry?

This is a question that I'm frequently asked, not only as a food writer and a vegan, but as someone who enjoys being able to cook low-effort meals, without having to make multiple trips to the supermarket.

Since I became vegan back in 2006, veganism has become much more mainstream, and many new-fangled and fad vegan-friendly ingredients have appeared on supermarket shelves, from vegan-friendly ingredients to vegan versions of our favourite brands, to plant-based ready meals. Many of these have come and gone, but there are ten core ingredients that have retained their spot in my store cupboard. These staple ingredients are the basis of nearly all my recipes for their versatility, cost-effectiveness, reliability, taste and availability. I'm so excited to share these ingredients with you in this book, with a chapter devoted to each of my ten 'hero' ingredients, and ten delicious recipes in each chapter to help you enjoy each ingredient to its full potential.

All of these ten ingredients are readily available and each recipe is cost-conscious. I've labelled which recipes are suitable for freezing, so you can save any leftovers for another day, or batch cook for your future self. Each recipe also contains an easy tip to help along the way.

There are now so many convenient vegan foods readily available, which is to be celebrated, as it opens veganism up to so many people. But convenience can come at a cost: financially, within your shopping bills, and to the planet, with wasted food and excess packaging. So, in this collection of 100 recipes, I've taken your shopping list back to basics with honest, sustainable ingredients to create hearty, delicious meals that everyone will love. The cooking methods are simple and easy, so are perfect for every night of the week.

MY TEN PANTRY STAPLE INGREDIENTS ARE:

OATS
Wholesome, hearty, versatile

CANNED TOMATOES
Simple, tasty, speedy

PULSES
Comforting, nutritious, accessible

CITRUS
Zesty, light, uplifting

PASTA
Easy, loved, filling

COCONUT MILK
Creamy, rich, handy

JACKFRUIT
Meaty, adaptable, satisfying

PEANUT BUTTER
Flavourful, powerful, convenient

TOFU
Complete, all-rounder, high-protein

GRAINS
Wholesome, nutty, heart-healthy

Whether you're a new vegan looking for a simple guide, a confident home cook looking for plant-based meals, or an established vegan in need of new ideas, I hope this book inspires you to cook with what you have available in your pantry, consider traditional ingredients alongside new ones, and create effortless vegan meals every day.

MY VEGAN PANTRY

These are the ten ingredients that I always have in my store cupboard, each of which has a whole chapter of recipes dedicated to it. With these to hand, I know that I can create healthy, balanced meals that are full of flavour, cost-effective, endlessly versatile and guaranteed to bring interest to your everyday meals.

OATS

Oats are one of the most commonly grown cereals in Britain, but despite their low cost and long shelf life they are often overlooked.

You may already regularly cook with oats in the mornings, for porridge with oat milk or granola, but oats have many uses, particularly in vegan cooking, including adding bulk to homemade vegan sausages, binding plant-based burgers, making crunchy crumble toppings, and packing baked goods with texture and nutrients.

Oats are high in fibre, particularly a soluble fibre called beta-glucan, which is thought to lower cholesterol. Oats are also a good source of protein, particularly when combined with other plant protein sources like beans and nuts. They are also rich in vitamins and minerals, and are a source of several B vitamins.

Oats are readily available in supermarkets. In this book, I've used rolled oats as they offer the most versatility in your pantry and can be used in many different ways. Rolled oats often have the longest shelf life – they can be stored in a cool, dry place for up to a year – and are quick to cook, as they are gently steamed during their production. All oat products begin as oat groats, and are then processed differently to produce different varieties. Others include steel-cut and stoneground oats, which have a longer cooking time; instant oats, which are fine and require very little cooking; and oat bran, which can be added to baking to increase the fibre content.

I wouldn't be without the humble oat. Their versatility in such a variety of dishes has earned them a permanent place in my pantry.

CANNED TOMATOES

Canned tomatoes are the base for so many recipes in vegan cooking and have been conveniently prepared so you can use them effortlessly. Canned tomatoes are a staple ingredient in many world cuisines, from Italian to Mexican, Indian to British. They can be used in sauces, casseroles, dips and soups, ranging from tangy and herby, to fiery and spicy.

Canned tomatoes have a similar nutritional profile to fresh ones; they have a high fibre content and are a good source of vitamins C and K. One particular benefit of canned tomatoes is the high content of lycopene, a powerful antioxidant that is released when they are cooked as part of the canning process.

'Canned tomatoes' is an umbrella term used for any preserved tomato in a can, bottle, tube or pouch. In this book, I've used canned chopped tomatoes, canned plum tomatoes, passata (sieved tomatoes) and tomato purée (paste). Canned chopped tomatoes are convenient, but if you prefer to control the chunkiness of your tomatoes, buy plum tomatoes and chop them as you like. Passata is made from sieved tomatoes to remove the skins and seeds, resulting in a smooth, sweet, rich sauce. Tomato purée is made from reduced cooked tomatoes, resulting in a thickened paste. It is highly concentrated; a small amount of purée adds a great burst of tomato flavour.

Canned tomatoes are one of the ingredients where quality really matters. Buy the best you can afford, and you'll really taste the difference. Keep a selection in your pantry so you can cook up something wonderful, with very little effort.

PULSES

Having a range of canned (and dried) pulses and legumes available means you can cook up a hearty dish in a few easy steps. Pulses are cost-effective and have a long shelf life, as well as being filling and comforting to eat. Pulses and legumes are the star of the show in so many traditional recipes from a range of cuisines, including hearty soups and stews. But thinking more broadly, there is so much you can do with beans and lentils, including speedy lunches, no-cook suppers, pies and one-pots. Not only are pulses easy to cook and delicious to eat, they are nutritional powerhouses, packed with protein and fibre; beans and lentils are also naturally low in fat.

In this book, I've used my favourite pulses, including cannellini beans, green and red lentils, chickpeas, red kidney beans, canned baked beans in tomato sauce, butterbeans (lima beans) and black beans. When choosing beans, for speed I always choose jarred or canned over dried, to save time and home energy, knowing they're ready to cook whenever I am. Dried beans take hours of soaking and boiling, whereas jarred or canned beans are pre-cooked and simply need draining of brine and rinsing in water. Jarred beans are generally of better quality (and larger) than canned, but do come at a higher price point, so use these when you really want your pulses to be the star of the show. Cooked lentils are conveniently available in cans or pouches, and quick-cook red lentils are best cooked from dried (they don't require soaking, simply rinse in cold water before cooking). It's worth noting that I use standard 400g (14oz) can sizes in the recipes in this chapter; when drained these will usually give you about 250-280g (9oz) drained weight of pulses, so do factor this in if you are using jars or pouches in larger sizes.

Jarred and canned beans and dried lentils are readily available in supermarkets. Keep them at room temperature until you need to use them, then enjoy them straight away and freeze any leftovers.

CITRUS

Lemons and limes are staples in my kitchen, taking my cooking to the next level, with an easy layer of fresh flavour and delicious aroma. But oranges and grapefruits are versatile too, in both sweet and savoury dishes.

If you've only ever added lemons and limes to drinks, or seen oranges and grapefruits as things to fill your fruit bowl, start thinking of citrus fruits as pantry staple ingredients, that will make your meals and baking zing. Use lemon to brighten slow-cooked dishes, lime to lift creamy curries, orange to flavour vegan yogurts, and grapefruit as the star of salads. Try a squeeze of lemon, orange or lime juice over your finished dish when you've removed it from the heat. This gives a layer of freshness and zing, without any bitterness.

Citrus fruits are known to be high in immune-boosting vitamin C and are packed with minerals and antioxidants. They are also high in fibre; however, this only applies if you're eating the flesh, not just drinking the juice.

In this book, I've showcased recipes to help you to get the most out of lemons, limes, oranges and grapefruits, as these are the most versatile, but other citrus fruits include yuzu, pomelo and kumquat and are worth looking out for and using in your cooking. When shopping for citrus fruits, it is important to always choose unwaxed varieties. Waxed citrus fruits are coated with an animal product, usually shellac (extracted from the lac insect) or beeswax, neither of which is suitable for vegans. The purpose of the wax is just to give the fruits a shinier, more attractive appearance, but I think you'll agree that unwaxed fruits look just as delicious! Store citrus fruits in the fridge or in a cool cupboard for longevity, but always bring to room temperature before using, to get the most juice out of the fruit.

Keep lemons and limes on your weekly shopping list so you've always got a quick way to elevate your cooking, and buy oranges and grapefruits for variation, or just enjoy as a simple snack.

PASTA

Pasta is a much-loved pantry essential, known for its versatility, speed of cooking, and because it's a delicious comfort food that the whole family will enjoy.

Not only is a packet of pasta perfect for throwing together with a quick tomato sauce, you can also use it to add substance to soups, bake one-pot suppers, and stir into salads. Different shapes are suited to particular dishes and sauces, but I'd absolutely encourage you to stock your pantry shelves with your favourites to suit your own preferences. My pantry almost always has a supply of dried orzo, penne, tagliatelle, pappardelle, macaroni, farfalle and lasagne, so I always have plenty of options.

In this book, the recipes all use dried pasta. Dried pasta is less likely to contain eggs than chilled, fresh pasta (but always check the ingredients!), which means that it is a long-life product, and so the perfect addition to any pantry. Try to buy the best quality you can afford; better-quality pasta retains its shape when cooked and holds the sauce more easily than cheaper versions. I'd recommend around 75g (3oz) dried pasta per person, but you can adjust this depending on how hungry you are and what else you're serving with it.

Dried pasta is known as a minimally-processed food, often made with just semolina flour and water. It is high in carbohydrates, making it the perfect food to give you energy when you need it! Wholewheat versions contain more fibre and have a sightly nuttier flavour, but may take a few minutes longer to cook. You can also find pastas made from lentils and chickpeas, which have a higher protein content, and these are often naturally gluten-free. I like to keep it simple, and usually use traditional dried pasta made from wheat semolina flour, for convenience and for that nostalgic taste.

Store dried pasta in a cool, dry space in your pantry for up to a year. It will keep well in its original packaging if sealed with a clip between uses, or you can decant into jars or containers. Cooked pasta that has not been coated in sauce can also be drizzled with olive oil and frozen for up to three months.

COCONUT MILK

Canned coconut milk is such a useful ingredient to keep in the pantry, for adding creaminess and richness to both sweet and savoury dishes. One of the most common uses of canned coconut milk is to cook up a delicious dairy-free curry, but this ingredient is so versatile, and can be used in silky smooth soups and smoothies, for tropical-tasting marinades, whipped into cream for desserts, and used for vegan no-churn ice cream.

Canned coconut milk is readily available from supermarkets but can vary in price between brands. If you're on a budget, always check the world food aisle at supermarkets, where you're likely to find it at a cheaper price. I've used full-fat canned coconut milk for the recipes in this book for the richness it brings to any dish; if you prefer, use a reduced-fat version, but expect less creaminess and flavour. Coconut milk is made by finely grating mature, fresh coconut flesh and combining it with water to create an opaque, snow-white milk. This milk is then treated with high heat to increase its shelf life and reduce the risk of spoilage. Small cans of coconut cream have a much higher fat content than coconut milk and a thicker, more solid texture – perfect for a concentrated hit of flavour and richness. Coconut milk in a carton (often found in the supermarket dairy milk aisle) is a thinner liquid with a higher amount of added water, making it an everyday alternative to cow's milk in hot drinks. Canned coconut milk should be stored at room temperature, as the naturally occurring cream will become solid and separate from the coconut water in colder temperatures.

Coconut milk is high in calories, so it supplies energy for activities throughout the day. It also contains medium-chain fatty acids, which are considered a healthier saturated fat. Like all fats, they should be considered in moderation but remain an important part of the diet. One of the most valuable medium-chain fatty acids in coconut milk is lauric acid, which is thought to be beneficial to skin health, as well as having anti-inflammatory and antimicrobial properties, to help your body fight infection.

JACKFRUIT

Whether you're a little bit curious or a die-hard fan, a can of jackfruit can transform a simple vegan meal into something special.

Canned jackfruit may still feel like a new mysterious ingredient, but rest assured it is simple to use, quick to cook, and delicious to eat. It has a naturally meaty texture, which means it's perfect for making vegan versions of dishes like pulled pork; in fact it can be used in any recipe where you want to substitute shredded meat, such as in a chilli or pot roast or for a home-cooked takeaway favourite like shawarma.

Jackfruit is a tropical fruit grown in South East Asia. Young, unripened jackfruit is canned at source as it has a versatile, meaty texture and a mild flavour – this is the type of jackfruit to keep in your store cupboard to use as a vegan meat. Look out for 'young', 'unripe' or 'green' jackfruit in brine or water (not sugar syrup!), to make sure you're not buying the ripened version, which has a much stronger, sweeter taste and is often dried into chewy snacks that have a distinctive flavour. You'll find canned young jackfruit in many supermarkets and Asian food stores, and the price varies between brands, but a 400g (14oz) can will feed 2-4 people when used in the recipes in this book. Make sure you drain and rinse canned jackfruit thoroughly, then pat it dry with kitchen paper or a clean tea towel before cooking. The small chunks can be halved or shredded easily by hand to the texture of your choice.

Due to the high fibre content of jackfruit, it is filling and substantial, as well as being naturally low in fat. It is not particularly high in protein, however, so be sure to combine it with some high-protein ingredients, such as pulses, grains, nuts and non-dairy alternatives, to make sure you are getting the protein you need.

Canned jackfruit is easy to store in your pantry, ready for flavouring in any way you fancy. This versatile, cost-effective ingredient is also less processed than other vegan meat alternatives, and cooks in minutes!

PEANUT BUTTER

If you thought peanut butter was just to spread on toast, think again! This handy ingredient can be used in so many different ways, for fast flavour in no time.

It's easy to think of peanut butter as just a jar of spread, but it makes a flavour-packed ingredient that brings richness to curries and stews, whisks up to make the perfect stir-fry sauce, acts as an all-important binder in vegan burgers, flavours beautiful bakes, and packs protein into breakfast smoothies.

Peanut butter is a supermarket staple, with the option of choosing a smooth or crunchy texture. Smooth peanut butter offers the best versatility across recipes; however; if you only have crunchy available, or if you just prefer it, it will add extra bite to any of the recipes. Peanut butter is made from ground, roasted peanuts, often with oils, sugar or salt added. Where possible, choose a version without added sugar so it can be used widely in savoury recipes. Palm oil is a common ingredient in peanut butter, so if you prefer to avoid it, choose a variety that uses sunflower or nut oil, or one that has a sustainably sourced palm oil. Other nut butters, such as cashew and almond, are delicious, particularly for snacking, but lack the richness and versatility of peanut butter as an everyday pantry ingredient.

Peanut butter is packed with protein and fibre, perfect for keeping you full throughout the day. It is also a good source of minerals, such as iron and magnesium, and vitamin E. Peanut butter (and peanuts) are naturally high in fats, including unsaturated fats; it's this high fat content that brings a creamy richness to dishes that lower-fat ingredients can't deliver.

Peanut butter is best kept at room temperature. Storing it in the fridge will make it hard to spoon out, and may separate the oils.

Keep a (big or small) jar in your pantry for essential snacking, full-on-flavour cooking and vegan baking.

TOFU

Tofu is a vegan staple that will surprise you with its versatility of uses. It soaks up flavours and can vary in texture depending on how you cook it, from crisp to meaty; it also makes a great base for creamy vegan desserts.

You may associate tofu primarily with Asian cuisines, but it can be used in so many dishes from around the world, including as an egg replacement in vegan quiche, scramble and frittata, as a meat alternative in burgers and sandwiches, and as a base to classic desserts.

Tofu is sold in varying levels of firmness, but in this book I have used pre-pressed extra-firm tofu and silken tofu. Extra-firm tofu is found in the chilled sections of supermarkets, vacuum-packed for freshness, and is solid with a spongy texture. Many supermarkets now sell pre-pressed extra-firm tofu, which means excess water has been drained from the tofu, so it is ready to use straight away. If your extra-firm tofu isn't pre-pressed, you can either use a tofu press, or simply wrap the block of tofu in kitchen paper or a clean, dry tea towel and place on a large plate. Place another plate on top of the block and add a couple of cookbooks or a heavy pan on top to weigh it down, allowing it to press for one hour. Silken tofu is sold in semi-liquid form, and is best used in desserts and sauces that require a creamy base. You'll find this on the pantry shelves in large supermarkets. There's no need to press this type of tofu, as its soft, creamy texture means you just use it straight from the carton.

Tofu is made from the curds of soya milk, similar to the way cheese is produced from dairy milk. It is a complete protein, which means that it provides all nine amino acids that the body needs. It is low in saturated fats and rich in minerals, including iron and zinc. Tofu is also a great source of calcium, with some brands boasting higher levels due to calcium-holding additives used.

Extra-firm tofu should be kept in the fridge, but most brands of silken tofu can be kept in the pantry at room temperature.

GRAINS

Many people add grains to their diet simply for the health benefits, but grains are also delicious, filling and comforting foods that provide so much more than nutrition.

There are so many things you can do with grains – instead of making them a side dish, celebrate their versatility and texture by making them the star of the show. Think risottos, stews and biryanis, to crispy toppings and nostalgic rice pudding.

There are many grains available in supermarkets, but in this book, I've chosen the most versatile options for recipes you'll want to make time and time again, including quinoa, wild rice, wheat (bulgur and couscous), basmati rice, pearl barley and pudding rice. (Although oats are also a grain, they're so fantastic that I had to dedicate a whole chapter to them!) These options are now readily available in shops, unlike grains such as teff, amaranth and millet, which can be a little harder to source. Grains are simple to use and don't require any special treatment other than a rinse in cold water, then cooking into your recipe. They are a relatively cheap ingredient to stock in your pantry and have a long shelf life. Cooking with grains is nostalgic and warming and can evoke memories, through aroma and taste, of family casseroles in times gone by, and, of course, sweet rice pudding.

Wholegrains such as quinoa, bulgur wheat, pearl barley and wild rice are packed with fibre, vitamins and minerals, and have a good amount of protein, too. White rice and couscous have less fibre (as the outer parts of the grain have been removed) but provide energy and are very versatile ingredients.

Store grains in airtight containers, in a cool, dark place in your pantry.

Grains are a store-cupboard staple, perfect for throwing together a speedy lunch or cooking up a filling, satisfying evening meal.

EXTRA INGREDIENTS

Alongside the ten staple pantry ingredients, make sure your fridge and cupboards are stocked with these ingredients too, to take your home cooking to the next level.

FRUIT AND VEGETABLES

Choosing seasonal produce means that you'll always have something new and different to cook with, to keep your meals varied throughout the year. Produce that is in season has the best flavour, and is cost-effective, whether you choose to buy it from the supermarket, greengrocer or local market. Frozen fruits and vegetables are a great way to enjoy your favourite fruit and vegetables out of season and are convenient to cook with. Try frozen butternut squash, spinach, leeks and – of course – peas, as a way to reduce food waste, by using only the amount you need and returning the rest to the freezer. Vegetables such as artichokes, sweetcorn and baby potatoes are preserved well in jars and cans, so you can enjoy them all year round (with minimal preparation) – see pan-fried artichokes with yogurt and crispy quinoa on page 225 for inspiration. Dried fruits like dates and apricots are versatile for use in both savoury and sweet dishes; try them in date, chickpea and lemon tagine (page 88) and pomegranate and apricot tabbouleh with black olives (page 220).

NON-DAIRY ITEMS

Have a selection of non-dairy items available, including your favourite plant-based milk, cheeses and yogurt. Soya or oat milks are the most versatile plant-based milks for cooking and baking and are available in most supermarkets. There are many varieties of vegan cheeses to choose from, but it's worth always having a soft, cream cheese and a hard, cheddar-style cheese on hand for cooking. Vegan yogurt not only makes a great snack, but is cooling on curries, and adds richness to breakfast bowls – thick, coconut yogurt is full of flavour, while vegan Greek-style yogurt is perfect for making creamy dips and sauces, such as aubergine fritters with orange harissa yogurt (page 82).

SEA SALT AND BLACK PEPPER

Use good-quality flaky sea salt for an enhanced flavour, or season with smoked sea salt flakes for extra depth of seasoning. Crush between your fingertips and scatter over your dishes. Freshly ground black pepper is bright and fruity, giving pops of gentle heat to season your finished dishes.

OILS

Oil transmits the heat from the pan to the food for faster, even cooking with no sticking. Sunflower oil and refined olive oil are excellent for cooking with, as they have no overpowering taste, and are versatile for roasting, frying and baking. Save extra-virgin olive oil (the more expensive option) for dressing salads and pasta, as it has a bright, peppery flavour that can be dulled when heated.

SPICES AND BLENDS

Build up a small collection of your favourite spices, and store them in a cool, dark space to preserve their flavour. Spice mix blends such as chilli powder and Chinese five-spice have been blended to create the perfect flavouring all in one jar, meaning they take up less room in your cupboard and require minimal fuss when cooking. Ensure curry pastes are vegan-friendly, as they can sometimes contain fish sauce or dairy milk. A mild or medium-strength curry paste, and a Thai green curry paste are excellent staples to have available for dishes such as cauliflower dhansak (page 45) and ginger braised mushrooms with coconut (page 132).

HERBS

Cook in flavour with woody herbs such as rosemary and thyme, or stir through bursts of freshness with fresh leafy herbs like flat-leaf parsley, coriander (cilantro), dill and chives. Woody herbs such as sage and oregano maintain a great flavour when dried, so keep a small selection of dried herbs in the cupboard. Store fresh herbs in a light, cool place, stems-down in a glass of water to extend their life.

FLOUR

Whether you're whisking up a white sauce for cauliflower mac and cheese (page 114) or baking summer fruit traycake (page 100), flour is an essential ingredient for any home cook. Have both plain (all-purpose) flour and self-raising flour available so you're ready to tackle any recipe, along with more specialist flours like gram and wholemeal, if you like.

SUGAR

Not only does sugar add sweetness to bakes and desserts such as coconut banoffee pie (page 142), but a pinch can eliminate any unwanted acidity in tomato-based dishes. For versatility, keep both white granulated sugar and soft light brown sugar in your pantry.

EQUIPMENT ESSENTIALS

Make cooking easy and effortless with these carefully selected equipment items. There's no need to fill your cupboards and worktops with the latest gadgets that you may rarely (or never!) use – keep it simple.

HOB-TO-OVEN DISH

A hob- and oven-safe lidded dish is versatile to use for any dishes that need to be started on the hob and then finished in the oven, without using additional pots and pans (saving you extra washing up). Cast-iron varieties are hard-wearing and last for years (I wouldn't be without my Le Creuset pans and dishes).

FREEZER-SAFE CONTAINERS

With the increasing costs of food and home energy, it's important not to waste food that you've cooked. Have a selection of freezer-safe storage boxes or resealable ziplock bags ready to spoon cooled food into, whether you're keeping your leftovers or batch cooking. Ensure they fit into your freezer and always squeeze out the air from a ziplock bag so it can lie flat in the freezer to take up as little space as possible. Your future self will thank you when you need a quick meal from the freezer! Look out for a 'suitable for freezing' symbol on the tried-and-tested freezer-friendly recipes in this book.

DEEP ROASTING TRAY

Standard baking trays are great for baking small goods, but a large, deep roasting tray allows you to cook a whole meal in one tray, taking full advantage of your oven. Coated non-stick, glass and ceramic stoneware versions transfer and hold heat evenly. Choose a roasting tray with deep sides to hold any liquids you add to the dish, to save on leaks and spills.

HIGH-POWERED BLENDER

Blenders are for so much more than making smoothies, allowing you to blitz soups, sauces and spice mixes with very little effort. Jug blenders often offer the highest quality and speeds and are easy to clean. Stick blenders are a great alternative for kitchens with less counterspace, although they will need more effort to blitz your sauces and soups to creamy smoothness.

KNIVES

A few good-quality kitchen knives make the task of chopping and slicing an effortless breeze. A small, medium and large knife and a serrated bread knife is enough, and I'd always recommend you choose knives that are comfortable to grip, with some weight to them, as this will make slicing easier. Care for your knives by always chopping onto a wooden board (instead of plastic or glass), as wood adds a little softness to protect the blade from wear and tear. Although a food processor can make chopping and slicing easier, it's by no means an essential, as a decent set of knives will do the same job.

PANTRY MENUS

Use these menu planners as a guide to get the most out of your pantry essentials, from family suppers to something special.

WEEKDAY

Cinnamon and hazelnut granola (page 28)

Lemon jackfruit baguette with mayo, chives and gherkins (page 152)

Summer fruit traycake (page 100)

Waffle-topped baked bean pie (page 70)

QUICK AND EASY

PB breakfast smoothie (page 184)

Quick grapefruit and fennel salad (page 87)

Easiest-ever weeknight tomato and chilli penne (page 118)

Two-minute mug crumble (page 34)

COMFORT SUPPER

Autumn roasting-pan soup (page 127)

Comforting leeks and lentils with lemon and ginger (page 69)

Fluffy coconut rice (page 131)

Easy pistachio, mango and coconut kulfi (page 145)

CELEBRATION SHARER

Pan-fried artichokes with yogurt and crispy quinoa (page 225)

Butterbeans in tomato, olive and caper sauce (page 51)

Aubergine lasagne al forno (page 121)

Limoncello tiramisu (page 96)

SATURDAY NIGHT FEAST

Store-cupboard salsa with no-waste tortilla chips (page 42)

Sweet and spicy cauliflower wings (page 173)

Loaded twice-baked potatoes with sticky BBQ jackfruit (page 160)

Chipotle black beans with sweet potatoes, pink pickled onions and chives (page 78)

SPECIAL SUPPER

Potato and onion tofu frittata (page 196)

Whole roasted celeriac with creamy mushroom wild rice (page 219)

Cacio e pepe-style butterbeans (page 74)

Crème brûlée (page 209)

BRUNCH SHARER

Toasted oat parfait with pomegranate and tahini yogurt (page 32)

Tofu bagels with pickled radish (page 194)

Blood orange pancakes with yogurt, maple and cinnamon (page 99)

Scrambled tofu on toast with mushrooms and tomato chutney (page 193)

WINTER WARMER

Pantry minestrone (page 106)

Roasted fennel, orange and leeks with Dijon cannellini beans (page 77)

Slow-roasted tomato, barley and bean stew (page 226)

Rum and raisin rice pudding (page 232)

OATS

TOASTED OAT TOPPER

MAKES 1 SMALL JAR

10 tbsp rolled oats

2 tbsp pumpkin seeds

2 tbsp sunflower seeds

2 tbsp blanched and chopped
    hazelnuts

1 tbsp sesame seeds

1 tsp garlic powder

pinch of chilli (red pepper) flakes

generous pinch of sea salt and
    black pepper

**Add a little flavour and crunch to soups and salads with this
simple toasted oat topper, which takes less than 10 minutes to
prepare. Store in a sealed jar in a cool place for up to a month.**

Add the oats, pumpkin seeds, sunflower seeds and chopped
hazelnuts to a dry pan over a medium-high heat and toast for
5-6 minutes until lightly golden and fragrant.

Remove from the heat and stir in the sesame seeds, garlic
powder, chilli flakes, sea salt and black pepper.

Allow to cool fully before spooning into a jar, or use straight
away as a soup or salad topper.

EASY TIP

To add a cheesy flavour to this mix, stir in 1–2 teaspoons
nutritional yeast flakes, or twist things up with 1 teaspoon
onion powder.

FOUR-INGREDIENT OATCAKES

MAKES ABOUT 12

150g (1½ cups) rolled oats

1 rounded tbsp vegan butter

generous pinch of sea salt

sprinkle of plain (all-purpose) flour,
   for rolling

Oatcakes are a tasty lunch or snack, as they are satisfying and filling. Serve with wedges of vegan cheese and your favourite chutney, with a spoonful of smoked houmous and chopped red onion, or simply with marmalade.

Preheat the oven to 180°C/350°F/gas mark 4 and line a baking tray with baking parchment.

Add the oats into a jug blender or food processor and blitz until the oats are roughly crushed, with some finer than others for extra texture. Set aside.

Melt the butter in a pan over a low heat, then stir in the sea salt. Remove the pan from the heat.

Stir the oats into the butter, then add 120ml (½ cup) lukewarm water. Allow to stand for a few minutes, then combine into a thick dough.

Dust a clean work surface with flour, then roll out the oat dough to a thickness of about 5mm (¼in). Use a 5cm (2in) cookie cutter to cut the oatcake into rounds, rerolling the dough scraps as needed.

Place the oatcakes onto the lined baking tray, then bake in the oven for 15 minutes. Allow to cool fully on a wire rack to become firm and crisp.

EASY TIP

Store the oatcakes in a sealed container and they will last for up to 5 days.

GOCHUJANG STICKY NO-MEATBALLS

SERVES 2

For the no-meatballs

1 x 400g (14oz) can of black beans, drained and rinsed

2 tbsp walnuts

2 rounded tbsp rolled oats

1 tsp dried mixed herbs

½ tsp dried sage

generous pinch of sea salt and black pepper

1 tbsp sunflower oil, for frying

For the sticky sauce

3 rounded tbsp orange marmalade

1 tbsp gochujang sauce (ensure vegan)

To finish

2 tsp sesame seeds

2 spring onions (scallions), finely chopped

small handful of fresh coriander (cilantro), torn

These no-meatballs are simple to make, with black beans, oats and walnuts. The chilli-orange glaze gives them a hot kick, with freshness from spring onions and coriander. Serve with rice, a crunchy salad, or in a sub bread bun with extra sticky glaze.

Dry the rinsed black beans on kitchen paper or with a clean cloth, then tip into a blender jug, along with the walnuts, oats, mixed herbs, sage, salt and black pepper. Pulse until semi-smooth, scraping the mixture down a few times with a spatula. Leave a few chunks remaining for texture.

Roll into 8 balls, using approximately 2 rounded teaspoons of the mixture per ball. Place onto a plate and cover with cling film (plastic wrap). Refrigerate for at least 6 hours, or overnight.

Add the oil to a frying pan over a low-medium heat. Add the no-meatballs and cook for 10–12 minutes, rotating once during cooking. Allow the edges to become browned before rotating. Place onto a plate when cooked.

Add the marmalade and gochujang sauce to a pan over a low heat. Stir frequently until combined into a sticky glaze.

Generously spoon the sticky glaze over the cooked no-meatballs or use a pastry brush to liberally coat each ball. When coated and glossy, scatter over the sesame seeds.

Use tongs to place the no-meatballs onto serving plates, then scatter over the spring onions and coriander.

EASY TIP

Gochujang sauce is a concentrated paste made with chillies, sticky rice and umami fermented soy. You'll find it available in many supermarkets, or Korean shops.

PUMPKIN, SAGE AND CHESTNUT CRUMBLE

SERVES 4

1 tbsp sunflower oil

700g (1½lb) pumpkin, peeled and diced into bite-sized pieces

1 red onion, roughly sliced

2 garlic cloves, crushed

1 rounded tsp dried sage

150ml (generous ½ cup) vegan double (heavy) cream

180g (6oz) cooked vacuum-packed chestnuts, roughly chopped

200g (1½ cups) plain (all-purpose) flour

3 tbsp rolled oats

2 rounded tbsp vegan butter

1 tbsp roasted pumpkin seeds

generous pinch of sea salt and black pepper

When you've finished carving those Halloween pumpkins, or can't resist the mini pumpkin arrangement this autumn, don't waste the delicious amber-hued vegetable; instead bake this savoury crumble with creamy, warming flavours and a crispy, toasted topping. Cooked chestnuts are available in most supermarkets, and save precious time roasting and peeling.

Preheat the oven to 180°C/350°F/gas mark 4.

Add the sunflower oil and pumpkin to a large hob-to-oven dish and cook over a medium heat for 4–5 minutes until the pumpkin begins to soften at the edges.

Add the onion, garlic and sage and cook for a further 2 minutes until fragrant.

Stir in the vegan cream and the chestnuts, then season with sea salt. Bake in the oven for 20 minutes.

Meanwhile, make the crumble topping. In a large bowl, mix together the flour and oats, then rub in the butter until it resembles chunky breadcrumbs. Stir through the pumpkin seeds and season generously with black pepper.

Remove the dish from the oven and spoon the topping over. Return the dish to the oven and bake for a further 20 minutes until golden and bubbling.

EASY TIP

If pumpkins aren't available, butternut squash makes a great alternative (including frozen butternut squash).

GARLIC MUSHROOM SAUSAGES AND CREAMY MASH

MAKES 6

For the sausages

2 tsp vegan butter

250g (9oz) chestnut (cremini) mushrooms, brushed clean and roughly chopped

3 garlic cloves, crushed

2 spring onions (scallions), finely chopped

generous handful of flat-leaf parsley, roughly chopped

6 tbsp rolled oats

3 rice paper wraps

1 tbsp sunflower oil, for frying

generous pinch of sea salt and black pepper

For the creamy mash

1kg (2lb 4oz) Maris Piper potatoes, peeled and evenly chopped

50ml (scant ½ cup) vegan double (heavy) cream

2 rounded tbsp vegan butter

small handful of fresh chives, finely chopped

generous pinch of sea salt

These homemade sausages are full of flavour, with a crispy skin and meaty texture. What's more, you know exactly what has gone into them, with no hard-to-pronounce additives. Rice paper wraps make the perfect vegan sausage skin and can be found in the world food aisle of supermarkets. Some rice paper wraps are made from tapioca flour, making them translucent, which is perfect for casing vegan sausages. Rice paper wraps are firm at room temperature so need to be softened in warm water for no more than 5 seconds before using to make them pliable. They can be a little delicate to handle at first, so ensure your work surface is oiled to make rolling the sausages easier. Serve with a vegan onion gravy, or a squeeze of ketchup, if you like.

To make the sausages, melt the vegan butter in a large pan over a medium-high heat and throw in the mushrooms. Cook for 4–5 minutes until fragrant, then stir in the garlic and spring onions and cook for a further 2 minutes, stirring frequently to avoid sticking. Remove from the heat and stir in the parsley. Set aside to cool for a few minutes.

Add the oats to a high-powered blender jug and blitz for a few seconds until they become finer. Add the cooked mushroom mix, season with salt and plenty of black pepper, then blitz again until a thick, coarse mixture is created.

For the creamy mash, put the potatoes into a large pan of salted water over a medium-high heat. Bring to the boil, then cook for 20 minutes until tender. Remove from the heat and thoroughly drain away the water, then allow the potatoes to stand for 2–3 minutes to release steam (this will ensure the fluffiest mashed potatoes).

While the potatoes are cooking, make your sausages. Fill a large bowl with warm (not hot) water. Brush a clean work surface or board with a little sunflower oil. Dip a rice paper wrap into the water for 3–5 seconds until it begins to soften. Remove from the water and place on the oiled work surface or board. Use a knife to slice the rice paper wrap in half.

Spoon 1 tablespoon of the blitzed mushroom mixture onto the centre of each half, spreading it down the length in a sausage shape. Roll the sides of the wraps in, then fold or twist the ends in, making a sausage shape. Repeat for each sausage.

Add the oil to a large frying pan and place over a low-medium heat. Add the sausages and cook for 12–15 minutes, turning frequently to avoid sticking and to give them an evenly crispy skin.

Return the potatoes to the pan and add the vegan cream and butter. Use a potato masher to combine and mash the mixture until your desired consistency

is reached. Don't forget to scoop potatoes from the outside of the pan into the centre to avoid large lumps. Stir in the chives and season with sea salt.

Serve the creamy mash and mushroom sausages on warmed plates.

EASY TIP

The sausage mix can be made up to a day in advance when kept in the fridge. For the crispiest skins, wrap the sausages in the rice paper just before cooking.

EASY TIP

The dumplings can be made a day in advance and kept
in the fridge until ready to use.

SOMERSET STEW WITH HERBY OAT DUMPLINGS ❄

SERVES 4

For the dumplings

100g (scant 1 cup) self-raising flour

70g (2½oz) vegetable suet

50g (½ cup) rolled oats

handful of flat-leaf parsley,
    finely chopped

pinch of sea salt and black pepper

For the stew

1 tbsp sunflower oil

1 leek, finely chopped

2 carrots, peeled and sliced into
    half rounds

1 tsp dried sage

200ml (scant 1 cup) good-quality
    cider (ensure vegan)

1 x 400g (14oz) can or jar of good-
    quality chopped tomatoes

2 x 400g (14oz) cans of
    butterbeans (lima beans),
    drained and rinsed

300ml (1¼ cups) hot vegetable
    stock

1 sprig of fresh rosemary

2 apples, thickly sliced

100g (3½oz) cheddar-style vegan
    cheese, grated

generous pinch of sea salt and
    black pepper

Beautiful Somerset in southwest England is famed for all things delicious, including apples, cider and tangy Cheddar cheese, to which you can now find great vegan alternatives. This is the ultimate autumn casserole, with butterbeans, apples, rosemary – and cider, of course. Oats give a homely flavour to the dumplings, which make the perfect topping to this comforting stew.

To make the dumplings, add the flour, vegetable suet, oats and parsley to a bowl. Season with a pinch of salt and plenty of pepper, then stir to combine. Gradually add 6 tablespoons cold water, bringing the mix together after each tablespoon to form a thick dough. Add a little extra water if needed, but the mix shouldn't be sticky. Use your hands to roll the mixture into 8 dumplings, then place them onto a plate and refrigerate until required.

Add the oil, leek, carrots and sage to a lidded hob-to-oven casserole dish and cook for 4–5 minutes over a medium heat until fragrant.

Pour in the cider and cook for another 2 minutes, then stir in the chopped tomatoes, butterbeans and stock. Finally add the rosemary sprig. Bring to the boil, then add the apple slices.

Simmer for 30 minutes, then remove from the heat. Discard the rosemary and season with salt and pepper.

Meanwhile, preheat the oven to 180°C/350°F/gas mark 4.

Lay the dumplings over the top of the stew and add the lid. Bake in the oven for 30–35 minutes until the dumplings have increased in size and the casserole is bubbling.

Carefully remove the lid, then scatter the cheese over the dumplings. Return to the oven without the lid for a further 10–15 minutes until the cheese has melted and the dumplings are golden.

CINNAMON AND HAZELNUT GRANOLA

MAKES 1 JAR

4 tbsp sunflower oil

4 tbsp maple syrup

300g (3 cups) rolled oats

generous pinch of ground cinnamon

50g (2oz) blanched hazelnuts, chopped

1 tbsp pumpkin seeds

2 rounded tbsp plump sultanas (golden raisins)

Homemade granola is surprisingly simple to make, and you can adapt the flavours and sweetness to your own taste. Prepare on a Sunday for a week of simple and delicious breakfasts, or snacks. Serve with thick coconut yogurt.

Preheat the oven to 160°C/320°F/gas mark 3.

Mix together the oil and maple syrup in a jug (pitcher).

In a bowl, combine the oats, cinnamon, hazelnuts and pumpkin seeds, then pour over the oil and maple syrup mixture. Stir together until everything is coated.

Spread the mixture out evenly over two baking trays, then bake in the oven for 40–45 minutes, stirring the mixture every 10 minutes to encourage oaty clumps to form. Remove from the oven and scatter over the sultanas while the oats are still hot. Allow to cool fully before transferring to a clean jar.

_____

EASY TIP

The granola will last for up to a month in a clean jar, when stored in a cool, dark cupboard.

BANANA, BLUEBERRY AND OAT MUFFINS ❄

MAKES 9

2 overripe bananas, peeled

50ml (scant ½ cup) sunflower oil

70g (2½oz) soft light brown sugar

150g (scant 1¼ cups) plain (all-purpose) flour

2 tbsp rolled oats, plus an extra 1 tbsp for topping

1 tsp baking powder

½ tsp ground cinnamon

½ tsp grated nutmeg

12 blueberries, halved

The ultimate rainy-morning treat, perfect for serving with a hot coffee. Let the soothing scent of brown sugar, banana and spices fill your kitchen – and your soul.

Preheat the oven to 180°C/350°F/gas mark 4 and line a muffin tray with paper muffin cases.

Use a fork to mash the bananas in a bowl, then stir in the oil and sugar until combined.

In a large bowl, stir together the flour, oats, baking powder, cinnamon, nutmeg and blueberries. Stir in the banana mixture and mix until just combined.

Add a rounded tablespoon-sized amount of the batter to each paper case, then scatter the remaining oats over the tops. Bake in the oven for 22–25 minutes until golden and risen.

EASY TIP

Don't overmix the batter, as this will give the muffins a tougher texture. For the fluffiest muffins, stir until the ingredients are just combined.

TOASTED OAT PARFAIT WITH POMEGRANATE AND TAHINI YOGURT

SERVES 2

8 generous tbsp rolled oats

2 tbsp shelled pistachios, roughly chopped

6 tbsp vegan Greek yogurt, chilled

1 tbsp tahini

1 tbsp maple syrup

seeds of 2 pomegranates

4 small fresh mint leaves, roughly torn

Sometimes you need a breakfast that is a little bit special, and this parfait is definitely worth getting out of bed for. Tahini gives vegan Greek yogurt a deliciously nutty and addictive flavour, perfectly balanced with juicy pops of pomegranate.

Add the oats and pistachios to a dry pan and toast over a medium-high heat for 4–5 minutes until light golden and fragrant.

Meanwhile, stir together the yogurt, tahini and maple syrup.

Set out two small dessert dishes or jars. Spoon in a layer of toasted oats, followed by the yogurt mix, then the pomegranate seeds, repeating until you reach the top of the jar. Finish by scattering over the torn mint leaves.

EASY TIP

If you don't want the messy task of deseeding a pomegranate, you can find chilled pomegranate seeds in supermarkets. Chopped fresh raspberries make a delicious alternative.

TWO-MINUTE MUG CRUMBLE

SERVES 1 VERY GENEROUSLY

3 tbsp plain (all-purpose) flour

3 tbsp rolled oats

3 tbsp demerara sugar

1 rounded tbsp vegan butter

generous handful of raspberries

generous handful of blackberries

1 tbsp caster (superfine) sugar

Need an emergency pudding? A quick fix of comfort food? This easy, speedy crumble cooks in just two minutes and the fruity filling is easily customizable – try grated apples, peaches, strawberries, or any soft fruits that you have in the fridge. Serve with a scoop of vegan vanilla ice cream, if you like.

Add the flour, oats and demerara sugar to a bowl and stir, then add the vegan butter and rub it in until the mixture resembles chunky breadcrumbs.

Fill a large mug halfway with raspberries and blackberries, then sprinkle over the caster sugar.

Spoon the crumble topping over the fruit, all the way to the top of the mug.

Cook for 2 minutes on high in an 800W microwave. Allow to cool for 2 minutes before enjoying, either spooned into a bowl or straight from the mug.

EASY TIP

Although the quantity of topping looks large, it does shrink a little when cooking in the microwave (and you can never have too much crumble...)

CANN

TOMA

ED

TOES

PROVENÇALE SOUP WITH PISTOU ❄

SERVES 4

For the soup

1 tbsp sunflower oil

1 medium leek, thinly sliced

2 carrots, thinly sliced into rounds

2 courgettes (zucchini),
    roughly diced

8 green beans, roughly chopped

2 garlic cloves, peeled and crushed

400g (14oz) good-quality passata
    (sieved tomatoes)

600ml (2½ cups) hot vegetable
    stock

1 sprig of fresh rosemary

1 sprig of fresh thyme

generous pinch of sea salt and
    black pepper

For the pistou

4 garlic cloves, peeled

generous pinch of sea salt

generous drizzle of olive oil

30g (1oz) pack of fresh basil

1 tbsp vegan cream cheese

Enjoy this herby soup in spring or early summer, as it is packed with fresh and seasonal ingredients. It is also perfect for batch cooking and freezing, to use up the summer vegetables and enjoy a taste of sunshine through to the autumn.

Heat the oil in a large pan, add the leek and carrots and cook over a medium-high heat for 5 minutes, stirring frequently to avoid sticking. Throw in the courgettes, green beans and garlic and cook for a further 2 minutes.

Pour in the passata and vegetable stock and stir through. Lay in the rosemary and thyme sprigs, then reduce the heat and simmer for 20 minutes.

Remove from the heat and discard the rosemary and thyme. Season to taste with salt and plenty of pepper.

To make the pistou, add the garlic, salt and olive oil to a food processor or high-powered blender and blitz until semi-smooth. Add the basil and cream cheese and blitz again until combined.

Ladle the soup into bowls and top each with a spoonful of the fresh pistou.

EASY TIP

The versatile pistou can be made a day in advance and kept in the fridge, but bring to room temperature before serving to bring out the best flavours. The pistou can also be drizzled through pasta, served as a dip with warmed crusty bread, or stirred through any casserole for a fresh, summery flavour.

TUSCAN-STYLE RIBOLLITA WITH ROSEMARY AND BEANS ❄

SERVES 4

1 tbsp olive oil, plus extra
   for drizzling

1 onion, finely chopped

1 carrot, chopped into half rounds

1 celery stick, finely chopped

2 garlic cloves, crushed

pinch of dried oregano

2 sprigs of fresh rosemary

1 x 400g (14oz) can of chopped
   tomatoes

1 x 400g (14oz) can of cannellini
   beans, drained and rinsed

800ml (3⅓ cups) hot vegetable
   stock

4 slices of thick white day-old
   bread, torn into small chunks

2 leaves of cavolo nero, tough
   stems discarded, leaves
   roughly chopped

generous pinch of sea salt and
   black pepper

few small basil leaves, to serve

This tomato-rich ribollita is one of my favourite comfort foods. Warming and herby, with plenty of white beans, it is thickened with leftover, day-old bread.

Add the oil, onion, carrot and celery to a large pan and cook over a medium-high heat for 5–6 minutes until softened. Add the garlic and oregano and cook for a further minute.

Add the rosemary, chopped tomatoes, cannellini beans and vegetable stock, then reduce the heat and simmer for 10 minutes, stirring occasionally.

Discard the rosemary sprigs, then stir in the bread and cavolo nero. Cook for a further 10 minutes until the bread has started to break down and thicken the stew.

Remove from the heat and season with salt and pepper. Drizzle over a little olive oil and ladle into warmed bowls. Scatter with a few basil leaves just before serving.

EASY TIP

This stew tastes even better on the second day, as the flavours mingle and the bread continues to thicken up the sauce. If you can resist finishing it on day one, you're in for a treat!

STORE-CUPBOARD SALSA WITH NO-WASTE TORTILLA CHIPS

SERVES 4

For the salsa

1 x 400g (14oz) can of chopped tomatoes

1 tbsp jarred jalapeño peppers, drained and roughly chopped

1 tbsp jarred chargrilled (bell) peppers, drained and roughly chopped

½ red onion, finely diced

pinch of chilli (red pepper) flakes

juice of ½ unwaxed lime

small handful of coriander (cilantro), finely chopped

generous pinch of flaky sea salt

For the tortilla chips

3–4 large white tortilla wraps, roughly sliced into triangles

1 tbsp sunflower oil

pinch of flaky sea salt

For those times when you need a satisfying snack, stir up this fiery salsa using store-cupboard ingredients and some fresh essentials for an extra zingy flavour. Use up any leftover tortilla wraps, even the ones that have started to harden at the edges, as they will become crisp and golden when baked. The salsa will last for up to 5 days in a fridge, while the tortilla chips will keep for 2–3 days in a sealed container in a cool cupboard.

For the salsa, add all of the ingredients to a bowl and stir to combine. Leave to stand for 15–30 minutes to allow the flavours to mingle.

To make the tortilla chips, preheat the oven to 180°C/350°F/gas mark 4. Arrange the tortilla triangles over 2 large baking trays, ensuring they don't overlap. Brush with the sunflower oil, then bake in the oven for 6–8 minutes until golden and crisp. Remove from the oven and sprinkle with sea salt.

Serve the tortilla chips warm or at room temperature, with the bowl of salsa to dip into.

_____

EASY TIP

For a milder salsa, soak the diced red onion in boiling water for 10 minutes, then drain away the water before adding the onion to the other ingredients. You can also reduce or leave out the chilli flakes.

CAULIFLOWER DHANSAK ❄

SERVES 4 GENEROUSLY

1 tbsp sunflower oil

1 onion, diced

1 carrot, diced

3 garlic cloves, crushed

2cm (¾in) piece of ginger, grated

½ tsp ground cumin

½ tsp ground turmeric

pinch of ground cinnamon

pinch of chilli (red pepper) flakes

1 rounded tbsp medium curry
    paste (ensure vegan)

1 x 400g (14oz) can of chopped
    tomatoes

1 tbsp tomato purée (paste)

600ml (2½ cups) hot vegetable
    stock

200g (1 cup) dried red lentils

1 small cauliflower, broken into
    florets, leaves discarded

1 rounded tbsp lime pickle

handful of spinach leaves,
    stalks discarded

generous pinch of sea salt

small handful of coriander
    (cilantro), torn

If you like your curries on the tangy, tomatoey side, this dish is for you. The perfect balance of acidity from the tomatoes and warmth from the spices alongside the creamy lentils is what makes this dish so delicious. Traditionally, dhansak has tamarind stirred in, but I like to use a spoonful of lime pickle, from the pantry, for a sour tang.

Heat the oil in a large pan, add the onion and carrot and cook over a medium heat for 2–3 minutes until starting to soften. Add the garlic, ginger, cumin, turmeric, cinnamon and chilli flakes and cook for a further 2 minutes.

Stir in the curry paste, then add the chopped tomatoes, tomato purée, vegetable stock and lentils. Bring to the boil, then simmer over a medium heat for 15 minutes, stirring frequently.

After 15 minutes, add the cauliflower florets and a splash of hot water, then simmer for a further 15 minutes until the lentils have broken down and the cauliflower is tender.

Stir in the lime pickle and spinach and cook for a further minute.

Remove from the heat and season to taste with sea salt. Scatter with the coriander just before serving.

_____

EASY TIP

Cook the red lentils down until they begin to melt and go soft for a smoother, thicker sauce.

BEST-EVER
PIZZA SAUCE ✳

MAKES ENOUGH FOR 4 PIZZAS

1 tbsp good-quality olive oil

4 garlic cloves, crushed

½ tsp dried oregano

1 x 400g (14oz) can of good-quality
    plum tomatoes

1 rounded tbsp tomato purée
    (paste)

½ tsp granulated sugar

generous pinch of sea salt and
    black pepper

Whether you cook your pizza outdoors in a wood-fired oven, or simply top a supermarket pizza base with all of your favourite toppings, every pizza deserves the very best pizza sauce. Using canned plum tomatoes allows you to create the smoothness of sauce you want, whether you like some chunks or prefer it completely smooth. Canned plum tomatoes also pack a flavour punch! I love to add fresh herbs to my pizzas but prefer to add them after cooking for prime freshness, colour and flavour.

Add the olive oil and crushed garlic to a pan and cook over a low-medium heat for 3-4 minutes until softened and fragrant (but not coloured), then stir in the oregano and cook for a further minute.

Pour in the plum tomatoes and tomato purée, then stir in the sugar. Use a fork or potato masher to break down the plum tomatoes to your preferred texture. Simmer for 30 minutes, stirring occasionally.

Remove from the heat, then season to taste with salt and black pepper.

_____

EASY TIP

Spoon the amount you need for one pizza into individual ziplock bags or reusable containers so you can simply defrost exactly the amount you need each time. No fuss and no waste!

TOMATO BAKED STUFFED CABBAGE LEAVES

SERVES 4 AS A SIDE DISH

500g (1lb 2oz) pre-cooked and
    cooled basmati rice

30g (1oz) mint leaves,
    finely chopped

generous handful of dill,
    finely chopped

generous handful of flat-leaf
    parsley, finely chopped

handful of chives, finely chopped

1 tbsp shelled pistachios,
    roughly chopped

juice of ½ unwaxed lemon

8 large savoy cabbage leaves

400g (14oz) good-quality passata
    (sieved tomatoes)

drizzle of olive oil

1 tbsp pine nuts

generous pinch of sea salt

These savoy cabbage leaves are stuffed with herby rice and pistachios, before being baked in smooth tomato passata. Don't miss out the pine nuts towards the end of cooking; they add a perfect toasted crunch! Serve alongside date, chickpea and lemon tagine (page 88) or with a slice of crusty bread.

Preheat the oven to 180°C/350°F/gas mark 4.

Spoon the rice into a large bowl and stir through the chopped mint, dill, parsley, chives and chopped pistachios. Stir in the lemon juice and season to taste with sea salt.

Lay out a savoy cabbage leaf on a clean surface. Spoon 3–4 tablespoons of the herbed rice into the centre of the leaf, fold the short sides inwards, then roll the long sides to seal. Place the stuffed leaf into a deep roasting pan and repeat until you've filled all of the leaves. Pack the stuffed leaves tightly next to each other.

Pour the passata around the stuffed leaves and drizzle the tops with olive oil. Cover the roasting pan loosely with foil and bake in the oven for 30 minutes.

Carefully remove from the oven and discard the foil. Scatter with the pine nuts and return to the oven for 5 minutes until the pine nuts appear toasted. Serve hot.

EASY TIP

Day-old cooked rice works well for this recipe, or use a pre-cooked rice pack, available in supermarkets. If you're planning to use day-old rice, ensure it is fully cooled and then refrigerated until use.

BUTTERBEANS IN TOMATO, OLIVE AND CAPER SAUCE ❄

SERVES 4

1 tbsp olive oil, plus extra
    for drizzling

2 garlic cloves, crushed

pinch of chilli (red pepper) flakes

pinch of dried oregano

100g (3½oz) pitted black olives,
    roughly sliced

2 tbsp jarred capers, plus 1 tbsp
    of the brine

400g (14oz) good-quality passata
    (sieved tomatoes)

pinch of granulated sugar

2 x 400g (14oz) cans of
    butterbeans/lima beans (or use
    jarred if you can find them)

generous pinch of flaky sea salt
    and black pepper

handful of flat-leaf parsley,
    chopped, to serve

If you're looking for a simple but satisfying midweek meal, these beans, inspired by Italian puttanesca sauce, are quick and easy to put together. Made vegan by swapping anchovies for capers, this beany twist on the traditional dish uses store-cupboard essentials and lets good-quality tomato passata be the star of the show.

Add the oil, garlic, chilli and oregano to a pan and cook for 2 minutes over a medium heat until fragrant.

Stir in the olives and capers, with the tablespoon of brine from the jar. Pour in the passata and sugar.

Stir in the butterbeans, then simmer over a medium-high heat for 10–15 minutes, stirring occasionally.

Remove from the heat and season with salt and pepper. Scatter over the parsley just before serving and drizzle with a little extra olive oil.

_____

EASY TIP

Serve these beans on toasted sourdough, with egg-free pasta or gnocchi, mashed potatoes, or simply on their own.

CHILLI AND CHOCOLATE ENCHILADAS ❄

SERVES 4

1 tbsp sunflower oil

1 onion, diced

1 yellow (bell) pepper, diced

2 tsp mild chilli powder

1 tsp smoked paprika

1 x 400g (14oz) can of chopped tomatoes

1 x 400g (14oz) can of red kidney beans, drained and rinsed

50g (2oz) dark (bittersweet) chocolate (ensure vegan), grated

1 tsp soft light brown sugar

8 soft tortilla wraps

generous pinch of smoked sea salt and black pepper

juice of ½ unwaxed lime

small handful of coriander (cilantro), torn

2 spring onions (scallions), finely chopped

Bake this hearty dish for a warming supper that everyone will love. Dark chocolate gives depth of flavour to the tomato base, with a comforting balance to the smoky spices. Serve with store-cupboard salsa (page 42). A family favourite that is great for batch cooking and freezing.

In a large pan, heat the oil, onion and yellow pepper over a medium heat for 4–5 minutes until softened. Stir in the chilli powder and smoked paprika and cook for another minute.

Pour in the chopped tomatoes and red kidney beans, then bring to a simmer. Stir in the grated chocolate and brown sugar, then simmer for 15 minutes. Season with smoked sea salt and black pepper.

Preheat the oven to 180°C/350°F/gas mark 4.

Spoon 6 rounded tablespoons of the tomato bean mixture into a high-speed blender jug. Add up to 50ml (scant ½ cup) cold water to loosen, and then blitz until semi-smooth. Set aside.

Lay a tortilla wrap on a clean, flat surface and add 3 tablespoons of the remaining tomato bean mixture to the centre. Fold in the sides and roll up, then place into a deep baking dish, seam side down. Repeat for all of the wraps, pushing each one close to the next so that the dish appears packed.

Pour the reserved tomato bean purée over the enchiladas, then bake in the oven for 30–35 minutes until the edges are golden.

Remove the enchiladas from the oven and drizzle over the lime juice. Scatter over the coriander and spring onions, then season with a little extra smoked sea salt, if you like.

EASY TIP

Feel free to add a handful of grated vegan cheese over the top of the sauce before cooking, or simply enjoy the smoky rich flavours with pops of fresh herbs and spring onions.

BAKED SWEET POTATOES WITH TOMATOES, OLIVES AND PEPPERS

SERVES 2

2 sweet potatoes, scrubbed clean

1 tbsp olive oil

1 x 400g (14oz) can of good-quality
    chopped tomatoes

1 garlic clove, crushed

pinch of chilli (red pepper) flakes

1 yellow (bell) pepper,
    roughly diced

8 cherry tomatoes

8 pitted black olives, halved

handful of flat-leaf parsley,
    finely chopped

generous pinch of sea salt and
    black pepper

handful of chives, finely chopped

1 fresh green chilli, sliced
    (optional)

Enjoy this all-in-one dish for lunch or as a light supper. Slowly bake sweet potatoes in tangy tomatoes, olives and peppers, with a hint of chilli and fresh herbs.

Preheat the oven to 180°C/350°F/gas mark 4.

Use a fork to prick the skins of the sweet potatoes, then rub over a little olive oil, about ½ tablespoon per potato. Place into a deep roasting tray, then bake in the oven for 45 minutes.

Meanwhile, add the chopped tomatoes, garlic and chilli flakes to a jug (pitcher) and stir together. Set aside.

Carefully remove the roasting tray from the oven and pour the chopped tomato mix around the sweet potatoes, but not over them. Add the yellow pepper, cherry tomatoes and olives to the roasting tray, then return to the oven for 15–20 minutes until the sauce is bubbling.

Remove from the oven and use a sharp knife to carefully halve each sweet potato. Place onto plates.

Season the sauce with salt and pepper, then stir in the parsley. Spoon generously over the sweet potatoes and top with the chopped fresh chives and green chilli, if using.

EASY TIP

Add a 400g (14oz) can of drained and rinsed cannellini beans if you're particularly hungry, or top with a little grated vegan cheese.

BAKED GNOCCHI WITH LENTILS ALLA BOLOGNESE ❄

SERVES 4 GENEROUSLY

1 tbsp olive oil, plus extra
    for drizzling

1 onion, diced

2 carrots, diced

2 celery sticks, diced

1 red (bell) pepper, diced

2 garlic cloves, crushed

1 tsp dried oregano

glug of red wine (ensure vegan)

1 x 400g (14oz) can of good-quality
    chopped tomatoes

1 x 400g (14oz) can of green lentils,
    drained and rinsed

1 tbsp tomato purée (paste)

pinch of granulated sugar

500g (1lb 2oz) shop-bought potato
    gnocchi (ensure vegan; see
    easy tip)

generous pinch of sea salt and
    black pepper

handful of small basil leaves,
    to serve

If you have vegan spaghetti bolognese on your weekly meal rotation, put a twist on the classic with this recipe using gnocchi instead. Potato gnocchi become golden and gently crisp when baked, perfect for absorbing all the flavours of this rich sauce. Serve with a wild rocket (arugula) salad, if you like.

In a large hob-to-oven pot, heat the olive oil, onion, carrots, celery and red pepper over a medium heat for 2–3 minutes until they begin to soften. Add the garlic and oregano and cook for another 2 minutes.

Pour in a generous glug of red wine and reduce for 2–3 minutes.

Pour in the chopped tomatoes, green lentils and tomato purée and stir in the sugar. Bring to a gentle boil, then reduce the heat and allow the sauce to simmer for 25–30 minutes, stirring frequently. Season to taste with salt and pepper.

Meanwhile, bring a pan of water to the boil and add the gnocchi. Cook until the gnocchi rise to the top, then drain away the water and set aside.

Preheat the oven to 200°C/400°F/gas mark 6.

Remove the bolognese from the heat and place the gnocchi just into the sauce, so the tops of the gnocchi are still visible. Drizzle the gnocchi with olive oil, then bake in the oven for 15–20 minutes until the sauce is bubbling and the gnocchi are golden.

Remove from the oven and scatter with small basil leaves just before serving.

EASY TIP

Many brands of shop-bought gnocchi are vegan, but do ensure it is free from eggs and milk before you buy. Look out for the ambient packs instead of the chilled varieties, which are more likely to contain animal ingredients.

PULS

E S

SMASHED WHITE BEANS ON TOAST WITH GRILLED NECTARINES AND HARISSA

SERVES 2

1 x 400g (14oz) jar or can of butterbeans (lima beans), drained and rinsed

small handful of flat-leaf parsley, finely chopped

drizzle of extra virgin olive oil

2 slightly underripe nectarines, halved, stone discarded

4 large slices of sourdough bread

2 tsp good-quality harissa paste

pinch of sea salt and black pepper

If you're looking at that punnet of nectarines that never seem to ripen, this is the perfect way to use them up. Prepare the smashed beans in advance, if you like, then bring to room temperature before using. A work-from-home lunch favourite.

Add the butterbeans to a bowl and smash with a fork until semi-smooth. Stir in the parsley and olive oil, then season with sea salt and black pepper. Set aside.

Place the nectarine halves on a griddle (grill) pan, cut side down. Grill over a high heat for 3–5 minutes until griddle marks appear and the fruit is hot. Remove from the pan and slice each half into 4 thick slices.

Grill or toast the sourdough until golden, then smooth the smashed beans generously over the toast.

Place the nectarine slices on top of the butterbeans, then drizzle with the harissa.

EASY TIP

For a flavour twist, switch the parsley for basil and the nectarines for peaches. Then drizzle with vegan pesto in place of harissa.

CREAMY CHICKPEA, SAGE AND KALE SOUP ❄

SERVES 4

2 onions, roughly chopped

1 potato, peeled and chopped

1 carrot, peeled and chopped

1 litre (4 cups) hot vegetable stock

2 tsp dried sage

1 x 400g (14oz) jar or can of good-quality chickpeas, drained and rinsed

2 generous handfuls of shredded kale, tough stems discarded

1 sprig of fresh rosemary

100ml (scant ½ cup) vegan double (heavy) cream

generous pinch of sea salt and black pepper

Comforting, creamy, and packed with goodness, this soup will warm your soul on those chilly days. It really benefits from being made the day before, as the flavours marry together and the rosemary continues to infuse the chickpeas. Your kitchen will smell like home!

Add the onions, potato and carrot to a pan, then pour in the vegetable stock. Bring to the boil over a high heat, then reduce the heat to medium and simmer for 20 minutes until the potatoes have softened.

Pour the mixture (including all the stock) into a high-powered blender jug, add the sage, then blitz until completely smooth.

Pour the smooth mixture back into the pan and add the chickpeas, kale and rosemary. Simmer over a low heat for 10–15 minutes until the rosemary has infused the soup and the kale has gently softened.

Remove from the heat and stir in the vegan cream. Season to taste with sea salt and black pepper.

EASY TIP

If you can, use jarred chickpeas for this recipe. They are often larger in size, more tender, and have a creamier flavour than their canned counterparts.

HERBY LENTILS WITH PITTA, PINE NUTS AND POMEGRANATE

SERVES 2 GENEROUSLY

2 tbsp pine nuts

1 tbsp olive oil, plus extra
  for drizzling

1 garlic clove, crushed

1 x 400g (14oz) can of cooked
  Puy (French) lentils (or use
  a pouch), rinsed

generous handful of dill,
  finely chopped

handful of flat-leaf parsley,
  finely chopped

2 large pitta breads

2 tbsp good-quality houmous

seeds of ½ pomegranate

generous pinch of sea salt

wedges of unwaxed lemon,
  to serve

This versatile mini-meal works as a brunch, lunch or light supper, as it is packed with protein, flavour and zingy fresh herbs. Puy lentils can be found in most supermarkets, sold pre-cooked in pouches or cans, and are a perfect addition to your pantry with their nutty aroma and al dente bite.

In a dry pan, toast the pine nuts for 2–3 minutes over a high heat, moving them regularly until fragrant – watch them carefully as they burn easily! Set aside in a bowl.

Return the pan to a low-medium heat and add the olive oil and garlic. Cook for 2–3 minutes until softened and fragrant. Add the lentils and stir through to coat them in the garlicky oil. Remove from the heat, stir in the dill and parsley, then season to taste with sea salt.

Toast the pitta breads until golden and hot and then smooth each with a generous tablespoon of houmous.

Load the herby lentils over the pittas, then scatter with the pomegranate seeds and the toasted pine nuts. Drizzle with a little extra olive oil and serve with wedges of lemon, for squeezing.

EASY TIP

If you have any of the herby lentils left over, add a squeeze of lemon juice and serve over a leaf salad the following day.

NO-COOK FAJITAS

SERVES 4

1 x 400g (14oz) can or jar of
  red kidney beans, drained
  and rinsed

250g (9oz) jarred chargrilled (bell)
  peppers, drained of oil and torn
  into strips

4 tbsp store-cupboard salsa (page
  42) or shop-bought salsa

handful of coriander (cilantro),
  roughly torn

juice of ½ unwaxed lime

4 large soft tortilla wraps

4 rounded tbsp vegan crème
  fraîche or vegan mayonnaise

1 large avocado, peeled and
  thinly sliced

½ small red onion, thinly sliced

4 leaves of baby gem lettuce,
  roughly shredded

few drops of Tabasco

generous pinch of sea salt

I love this supper on a summer evening, when it's too warm to be in the kitchen (and you don't want to have the oven or hob on!). Vegan crème fraîche is available in supermarkets; it is usually oat based and perfect for adding a tangy yet cooling flavour. If you don't have vegan crème fraîche available, substitute with vegan mayonnaise. Serve with tortilla chips, if you like.

In a large bowl, stir together the beans, peppers, salsa and coriander, mashing a few of the beans with a spoon. Stir in the lime juice and season with a pinch of sea salt.

Lay out the tortilla wraps and spread a tablespoon of vegan crème fraîche over each one.

Lay over the avocado, red onion and lettuce, then generously spoon over the bean mix.

Sprinkle over a few drops of Tabasco sauce to taste, then fold the wraps and cut in half.

EASY TIP

You'll find jarred chargrilled peppers with antipasti ingredients in most supermarkets. They are quick and versatile to use – a perfect pantry staple.

COMFORTING LEEKS AND LENTILS WITH LEMON AND GINGER ❄

SERVES 4

1 tbsp sunflower oil

2 leeks, finely chopped

2 garlic cloves, crushed

4cm (1½in) piece of ginger, finely grated

pinch of chilli (red pepper) flakes

½ tsp ground turmeric

½ tsp ground cumin

1 tbsp medium curry paste (ensure vegan)

400g (14oz) dried red lentils, rinsed

1 litre (4 cups) hot vegetable stock

1 unwaxed lemon, at room temperature

generous handful of coriander (cilantro), finely chopped

generous pinch of sea salt and black pepper

4 tbsp coconut yogurt, to serve

This has become my ultimate comfort food, simply eaten with a spoon from the bowl, or served like a dhal with fluffy basmati rice. It's wonderfully warming on cold winter days, especially when seasonal colds and flu set in.

Add the oil and leeks to a large pan and cook over a medium-high heat for 5 minutes until softened and fragrant. Add the garlic, ginger, chilli flakes, turmeric and cumin and cook for a further 2 minutes, stirring frequently.

Stir in the curry paste, then add the lentils and vegetable stock. Bring to the boil, then reduce the heat to medium and cook for 25 minutes, stirring often to avoid sticking.

When the lentils have softened and broken down, remove the pan from the heat. Squeeze in the juice of the lemon and stir through the coriander. Season to taste with salt and pepper.

Serve in warmed bowls, with a spoonful of cooling coconut yogurt on top.

EASY TIP

This recipe is perfect for batch cooking and freezing into individual containers. Freeze for up to 3 months and defrost before reheating in a microwave or pan until piping hot.

WAFFLE-TOPPED BAKED BEAN PIE

SERVES 4

1 tbsp sunflower oil

1 onion, finely diced

1 red (bell) pepper, diced

1 tsp mild chilli powder

1 tsp smoked paprika

1 x 400g (14oz) can of chopped
tomatoes

2 x 400g (14oz) cans of baked
beans in tomato sauce

1 tbsp barbecue sauce
(ensure vegan)

6 frozen potato waffles, or enough
mini waffles to cover the pie
completely

generous pinch of sea salt

If you're looking for a fun and easy family dinner, look no further than this 'cheat's pie'. A gently spiced, beany filling is baked and topped with potato waffles – the fastest potato pie topping! Serve with corn on the cob and you'll have clean plates all round.

Add the oil, onion and red pepper to a pan over a medium-high heat and cook for 2–3 minutes until the onion begins to soften. Stir in the chilli powder and smoked paprika.

Pour in the chopped tomatoes, baked beans in tomato sauce and the barbecue sauce. Stir to combine, then simmer for 15 minutes.

Preheat the oven to 180°C/350°F/gas mark 4.

Season the beany filling with salt, then spoon into a large ovenproof dish (a lasagne dish is ideal). Lay over the waffles to cover the top of the pie and bake in the oven for 20–25 minutes until the waffles are golden. Serve hot.

EASY TIP

Choose from standard frozen potato waffles, mini potato waffles, or even hash brown waffles, now available in large supermarkets. Always check that the potato waffles are vegan, although most varieties are.

SPEEDY GREENS
AND BEANS

SERVES 2 GENEROUSLY

1 tbsp olive oil, plus extra
   for drizzling

1 leek, finely chopped

1 courgette (zucchini), sliced into
   half rounds

3 generous handfuls of shredded
   kale, tough stems discarded

1 garlic clove, crushed

1 x 400g (14oz) jar or can of
   cannellini beans, drained
   and rinsed

handful of mint leaves,
   finely chopped

generous handful of chives,
   finely chopped

juice of 1 unwaxed lemon

generous pinch of sea salt and
   black pepper

Combine creamy beans with vibrant green vegetables, fresh mint and chives for the perfect light meal for warmer days. Delicious served in a bowl with crusty bread, or over a thick slice of toasted sourdough, this is a lovely supper for when it's too hot to spend ages in the kitchen.

Heat the oil in a pan and add the leek and courgette. Cook over a medium-high heat for 4–5 minutes, then stir in the kale and garlic and cook for a further 2 minutes until fragrant and softened.

Stir in the cannellini beans and cook for a few minutes until hot.

Remove from the heat and stir in the mint and chives.

Pour in the lemon juice, then season to taste with salt and plenty of pepper. Serve in bowls with an extra drizzle of olive oil, if you like.

EASY TIP

Creamy cannellini beans are perfect for this recipe, but you could use butterbeans (lima beans), edamame beans or broad (fava) beans.

CACIO E PEPE-STYLE BUTTERBEANS

SERVES 2 GENEROUSLY

50g (2oz) vegan butter

50g (2oz) plain (all-purpose) flour

500ml (2 cups) unsweetened soya or oat milk

200g (7oz) hard cheddar-style vegan cheese, grated

1 x 600g (21oz) jar of giant butterbeans (lima beans), drained and rinsed

sea salt and black pepper

Add a classic Italian twist to butterbeans, by baking them in a cheese and black pepper sauce. If you can, use a jar of giant, or queen, butterbeans, as they are creamier and more flavoursome than their canned counterparts. Serve with a fresh green salad, toasted sourdough, or simply in a bowl with a spoon.

Preheat the oven to 200°C/400°F/gas mark 6.

Add the butter to a pan and gently melt over a low heat. Stir in the flour and keep stirring until a thick paste (roux) is created. Cook for a further 2 minutes.

Using a balloon whisk, gradually pour over the milk, whisking as you go. If the mixture appears to separate or split, whisk until it comes together before adding any more milk. Once all of the milk is added, whisk continuously for 5–6 minutes and keep the pan on the heat until you have a thick, smooth sauce.

Remove from the heat and fold in the grated cheese, then season with a pinch of salt and plenty of black pepper.

Stir in the butterbeans, then pour into an ovenproof dish.

Bake in the oven for 20–25 minutes until golden and bubbling.

EASY TIP

Jarred butterbeans work best in this dish, but if you only have canned butterbeans available, rinse them in boiling water to soften before using. You can also switch the dish up with cannellini beans, if you like.

ROASTED FENNEL, ORANGE AND LEEKS WITH DIJON CANNELLINI BEANS

SERVES 4

1 large fennel bulb, sliced into 8 wedges

2 unwaxed oranges, peeled and sliced into half rounds

2 leeks, sliced into roughly 3cm (1¼in) pieces

olive oil, for drizzling

1 x 400g (14oz) can or jar of cannellini beans, drained and rinsed

2 tsp Dijon mustard

½ tsp fennel seeds

1 unwaxed lemon, halved

generous pinch of sea salt and black pepper

Treat yourself to an effortless, roasting-pan supper with fragrant fennel, bitter roasted orange and just-crispy cannellini beans. Dijon mustard brings a creamy heat to the beans, with a moreish tang. Perfect served in a bowl, or with buttery mashed potatoes with chives.

Preheat the oven to 180°C/350°F/gas mark 4.

Arrange the fennel, oranges and leeks over 2 large roasting trays and drizzle with olive oil. Roast in the oven for 20 minutes.

Meanwhile, add the cannellini beans to a bowl and stir in the mustard, fennel seeds and the juice of half of the unwaxed lemon (reserve the other half for later). Stir in another drizzle of olive oil.

Carefully remove the roasting trays from the oven and spoon the beans around the vegetables. Return the trays to the oven for a further 10–12 minutes until the vegetables are browned at the edges and some of the beans are crispy.

Squeeze over the remaining lemon juice and season generously with salt and black pepper just before serving.

EASY TIP

Spread the ingredients across two roasting trays rather than packing them into one, so the ingredients have space to roast. If the ingredients are too close to each other, they will steam and become soggy instead of crisp at the edges.

CHIPOTLE BLACK BEANS WITH SWEET POTATOES, PINK PICKLED ONIONS AND CHIVES ❄

SERVES 4

For the pink pickled onions

1 large red onion, thinly sliced into half rounds

6 tbsp cider vinegar

generous pinch of chilli (red pepper) flakes

generous pinch of sea salt

For the chipotle black beans

1 tbsp sunflower oil

1 sweet potato, peeled and chopped into bite-sized pieces

2 Ramiro peppers, sliced

2 garlic cloves, crushed

1 tsp smoked paprika

½ tsp dried oregano

1 rounded tsp chipotle paste (ensure vegan)

1 x 400g (14oz) can of chopped tomatoes

1 x 400g (14oz) can or jar of black beans, drained and rinsed

pinch of sea salt

2 rounded tbsp vegan crème fraîche

handful of chives, finely chopped

Warm your body and soul with these smoky, spicy black beans and sweet potatoes. Use Ramiro peppers in this recipe if you can, as they have a softer skin than bell peppers and become addictively slippery when cooked. If you only have bell peppers available, be sure to slice them very thinly. Serve in warmed bowls with a few tortilla chips, or with a helping of rice, if you like.

Place the sliced red onion in a heatproof bowl and pour over enough cold water to cover the onion. Microwave on high for 5 minutes, then carefully drain away the water. (Alternatively, add the sliced onion to a pan of boiling water and simmer for 10 minutes, then drain.) Pour over the cider vinegar, then stir in the chilli flakes and sea salt. Leave to stand for at least 30 minutes, until the onions are bright pink.

Add the oil to a large pan and add the sweet potato and peppers. Cook over a medium-high heat for 5–6 minutes, stirring frequently, until they start to soften with some blackening at the edges.

Reduce the heat slightly and add the garlic, smoked paprika and oregano. Cook for 1 minute, then stir in the chipotle paste.

Pour in the chopped tomatoes and black beans, then simmer for 30 minutes, stirring frequently. Season to taste with sea salt.

Ladle into warmed bowls, then spoon over the crème fraîche, about ½ tablespoon per bowl. Scatter over the chives, then spoon over the pink pickled onions,

---

EASY TIP

Vegan crème fraîche is available in supermarkets and is often oat based. Use it to cool spicy foods, stir through mashed potatoes, or as a sauce for a pizza bianco.

CITR

US

AUBERGINE FRITTERS WITH ORANGE HARISSA YOGURT

SERVES 4

For the fritters

200ml (scant 1 cup) sunflower oil, for frying

100g (¾ cup) plain (all-purpose) flour

50g (½ cup) cornflour (cornstarch)

½ tsp baking powder

pinch of sea salt

200ml (scant 1 cup) ice-cold sparkling water

2 medium aubergines (eggplants), thinly sliced into half circles

For the orange harissa yogurt

3 rounded tbsp vegan Greek yogurt, chilled

zest and juice of ½ unwaxed orange

1 tsp rose harissa paste

pinch of sea salt

These hot aubergine fritters are coated in a light-as-air batter, perfect as a lunch or light nibble. Serve with a bowl of the orange harissa yogurt, for generous dipping.

Begin to heat the oil in a large pan while you prepare the batter.

In a wide bowl, combine the flour, cornflour, baking powder and sea salt. Stir in the sparkling water and use a balloon whisk to gently beat until smooth.

Dip the aubergine slices into the batter and shake off any excess. Using a slotted spoon, add a few slices of aubergine to the very hot oil. Deep-fry for 2–3 minutes until the batter has become crisp and puffed.

Carefully remove from the hot oil and drain on kitchen paper while you cook the remaining aubergine slices.

To make the orange harissa yogurt, mix together the yogurt, orange zest and juice, then swirl in the harissa. Season to taste with sea salt. Serve in a dipping bowl alongside the hot aubergine fritters.

EASY TIP

The orange harissa yogurt dip can be made a day in advance and kept in the fridge until ready to use. Refresh the dip with a quick squeeze of orange before serving.

MEXICAN-STYLE SWEETCORN SOUP WITH CHILLI AND LIME ✳

SERVES 4

1 tbsp sunflower oil

1 onion, diced

1 small red chilli, deseeded and
    finely chopped

1 red (bell) pepper, diced

1 garlic clove, crushed

1 tsp smoked paprika

2 x 198g (7oz) cans of sweetcorn
    (or use frozen sweetcorn),
    drained

1 x 400ml (14fl oz) can of full-fat
    coconut milk

600ml (2½ cups) hot vegetable
    stock

zest and juice of 2 unwaxed limes

generous pinch of smoked sea salt

1 spring onion (scallion),
    finely chopped

small handful of coriander
    (cilantro) leaves, torn

**Inspired by the smoky, sweet flavours of Mexican street
corn, this soup is packed with the fresh taste of limes.
This freshness brings out the naturally buttery flavour of
sweetcorn – either canned or frozen works well for this recipe.**

Heat the oil, onion, chill and red pepper in a large pan over a
medium heat for 4–5 minutes until the onion begins to soften.
Stir in the garlic and smoked paprika and cook for a further
2 minutes.

Pour in the sweetcorn, coconut milk and stock and bring to
the boil, then simmer over a low-medium heat for 20 minutes.

Remove from the heat, then ladle half of the soup into a
high-powered blender jug and blitz until smooth, then return
it to the pan and stir back through.

Scatter in the lime zest and stir in the lime juice, then season to
taste with a pinch of smoked sea salt. Ladle into warmed bowls
and serve scattered with the spring onion and coriander.

EASY TIP

To ramp up the hot smoked chilli flavour, add 1 teaspoon
chipotle paste along with the garlic and smoked paprika.

QUICK GRAPEFRUIT AND FENNEL SALAD

SERVES 2 GENEROUSLY

1 small fennel bulb, thinly sliced

2 unwaxed grapefruits, peeled and segmented

1 avocado, diced

1 tbsp pumpkin seeds

1–2 handfuls of watercress

juice of 1 unwaxed lemon

1 tsp poppy seeds

½ tsp ground sumac

pinch of sea salt

This quick and easy salad is my go-to recipe for a warm day, when you just want something simple and fresh. Fennel adds crunch and balances out the bitter grapefruit, but it can be switched for thinly sliced red cabbage, if you prefer.

In a large bowl, toss together the fennel, grapefruit, avocado, pumpkin seeds and watercress.

In a separate bowl, stir together the lemon juice, poppy seeds, sumac and sea salt.

Pour the dressing into the salad bowl and combine until coated. Serve on individual plates or as a sharing bowl.

EASY TIP

Sumac is a spice known for its zingy, citrus flavour. It adds another layer of freshness to this salad and can also be added to tagines, soups and roasted vegetables.

DATE, CHICKPEA AND LEMON TAGINE ❄

SERVES 4 GENEROUSLY

3 tbsp olive oil

1 red onion, roughly quartered

2 garlic cloves, peeled

3cm (1¼in) piece of ginger, peeled

2 tsp ground cumin

1 tsp ground turmeric

1 tsp harissa paste

2 tbsp maple syrup

3 carrots, peeled and roughly chopped into 3cm (1¼in) pieces

2 sweet potatoes, peeled and roughly chopped into 3cm (1¼in) pieces

2 parsnips, peeled and roughly chopped

1 brown onion, quartered

1 x 400g (14oz) can or jar of chickpeas, drained and rinsed

10 dates, pitted

juice of 1 unwaxed lemon

generous pinch of sea salt and black pepper

handful of flat-leaf parsley, roughly chopped

This spiced, slow-cooked tagine is filling and fruity, with the all-essential freshness of lemon juice awakening all of the flavours. Squeeze it over after cooking to avoid any overly bitter flavour; it will brighten the whole dish. For an extra lemony zing, stir through some chopped easy preserved lemons (page 95) before cooking.

Preheat the oven to 180°C/350°F/gas mark 4.

Add 2 tablespoons of the oil, the red onion, garlic, ginger, cumin, turmeric, harissa and maple syrup to a high-powered blender jug, along with 200ml (scant 1 cup) cold water. Blitz until smooth, then set aside.

Add the remaining tablespoon of oil to a lidded hob-to-oven dish and add the carrots, sweet potatoes, parsnips and brown onion. Cook over a medium-high heat for 5 minutes until the edges start to soften.

Remove from the heat and pour over the chickpeas. Stir in the blended spice mix, then arrange the dates over the top. Cover the dish with the lid.

Bake in the oven for 40 minutes, then reduce the heat to 160°C/320°F/gas mark 3 and cook for a further 15 minutes.

Remove from the oven and generously drizzle over the lemon juice. Season with salt and pepper and scatter over the flat-leaf parsley before serving.

EASY TIP

Switch the dates for dried apricots, if you prefer.

10-MINUTE THAI-STYLE FRIED RICE ❄

SERVES 2

1 tbsp sunflower oil

2 garlic cloves, crushed

2cm (¾in) piece of ginger, grated

1 red chilli, thinly sliced

6 sugarsnap (snap) peas, halved

6 stems of Tenderstem broccoli
   (broccolini)

200g (½ cup) cooked jasmine or
   basmati rice

generous splash of dark soy sauce

4 spring onions (scallions),
   finely chopped

juice of 1 unwaxed lime

handful of fresh coriander
   (cilantro), roughly torn

2 tsp black sesame seeds

If you cook up too much rice, don't let it go to waste. This Thai-style fried rice is a lighter, fresher take on classic fried rice, with plenty of ginger and lime. For extra heat, drizzle with a little sriracha before serving, if you like.

Add the oil to a wok over a medium heat; when hot, add the garlic, ginger and chilli and let it all infuse for 2 minutes – you don't want the garlic to colour.

Throw in the sugarsnap peas and broccoli stems and stir-fry for 2–3 minutes. Spoon in the rice and then stir in the soy sauce. Cook for 5 minutes until piping hot, stirring frequently to coat the rice in the infused oil.

Remove from the heat and stir in the spring onions and lime juice. Scatter over the coriander and black sesame seeds and serve.

EASY TIP

To make this fried rice stretch further, crumble in a 280g (9oz) block of pre-pressed firm tofu along with the sunflower oil and cook for 5 minutes, then continue with the recipe as above.

WARM ROOTS SALAD WITH BLOOD ORANGE AND THYME

SERVES 4

6 parsnips, peeled and thickly chopped

3 carrots, peeled and thickly chopped

400g (14oz) baby potatoes, halved

2 red onions, quartered

2 sprigs of fresh thyme

generous drizzle of olive oil

2 large unwaxed blood oranges, peeled

1 head of radicchio, leaves roughly torn

generous pinch of sea salt and black pepper

This winter salad is a fresher alternative to warming winter stews and casseroles, while still celebrating the produce of the season. Blood oranges and radicchio give a bitter balance to sweet, slow-roasted root vegetables, peppered with thyme.

Preheat the oven to 180°C/350°F/gas mark 4.

Arrange the parsnips, carrots, potatoes and red onions in a large roasting tray, or over two smaller roasting trays.

Scatter over the leaves of one sprig of thyme and lay the other whole sprig over the top. Drizzle with olive oil, then roast in the oven for 40–45 minutes until the vegetables are golden and crisp, and softened on the inside.

Meanwhile slice the blood oranges, saving one half of a blood orange for juicing.

Remove the roasted vegetables from the oven and discard the whole thyme sprig. Spoon into a large bowl and toss in the sliced blood orange. Squeeze over the juice of the remaining blood orange half.

Add the radicchio leaves and toss to distribute. Season with sea salt and black pepper before serving.

EASY TIP

This salad is created to be eaten warm, but it also tastes delicious served chilled the following day as part of a leafy salad.

EASY PRESERVED LEMONS

MAKES 1 LARGE (500ML/17FL OZ) JAR

8 medium-sized unwaxed lemons,
   scrubbed clean

200g (7oz) flaky sea salt

handful of black peppercorns

2 bay leaves

Preserved lemons are a store-cupboard delight. Add a spoonful to a tagine, to houmous, or even stirred through pasta for a salty-sweet flavour. It's surprisingly easy to make your own preserved lemons at home and they are perfect for dipping into throughout winter.

Sterilize your jar carefully (see easy tip, below).

Slice each lemon in half lengthways, then slice each half into 3 thick strips.

Scatter half of the salt onto a plate and press each piece of lemon into the salt to coat it.

Tightly pack the lemons into the jar, pressing the remaining salt around each piece as you go.

Add the peppercorns and bay leaves over the top, along with a final scattering of salt.

Securely add the lid and give the jar a shake. Place in a dark, cool place for around 3 months, shaking daily.

EASY TIP

A Kilner or mason jar is ideal for this recipe and will need to be sterilized before use. Either handwash the jar and lid thoroughly, or run through a dishwasher, then dry completely in a very low oven at 140°C/280°F/gas mark 1.

LIMONCELLO TIRAMISU

SERVES 8

For the lemon curd drizzle

zest and juice of 2 unwaxed
 lemons

75g (generous ½ cup) caster
 (superfine) sugar

200ml (scant 1 cup) soya or
 oat milk

1 tbsp cornflour (cornstarch)

For the lemon sponge fingers

125g (1 cup) self-raising flour

50g (½ cup) caster (superfine)
 sugar

½ tsp baking powder

125ml (½ cup) soya or oat milk

zest of 1 unwaxed lemon

To assemble

6 tbsp limoncello

500ml (2 cups) plant-based
 double (heavy) cream

2 tbsp shelled pistachios,
 finely chopped

**This light, summery twist on tiramisu celebrates all things
lemon: using the zest, juice and, of course, limoncello. This
grown-up dessert is traditionally sliced into square portions,
but it can also be served in individual ramekin dishes, or
simply by the spoonful.**

To make the lemon curd drizzle, add the lemon zest and juice,
the sugar and plant-based milk to a pan. In a small bowl or cup,
mix the cornflour with 2 tablespoons tepid water and mix into a
paste, then pour this into the pan. Bring the pan to the boil over
a medium heat while whisking with a balloon whisk, then reduce
the heat and simmer for 20 minutes, whisking frequently. Allow
to cool and thicken, then pour into a bowl or jug (pitcher), cover
and refrigerate for 4 hours, or overnight.

Preheat the oven to 180°C/350°F/gas mark 4 and line an 18cm
(7in) square cake tin with baking parchment.

In a bowl, stir together the flour, sugar and baking powder.
Pour in the plant-based milk and mix until just combined into a
smooth batter. Stir in the lemon zest and pour into the prepared
cake tin, then bake for 15–18 minutes until golden and springy
to touch.

Remove from the oven and allow to cool in the tin. When the
sponge has cooled fully, slice into fingers around 5cm (2in)
in length.

Pour the limoncello into a shallow dish, then dip each sponge
finger into the limoncello, turning it so it is soaked on each side.
Repeat with all of the sponge fingers, placing them into the
bottom of a serving dish or individual dishes. Drizzle the soaked
sponge fingers with half of the chilled lemon curd.

Pour the double cream into a bowl, then use a hand-held
electric whisk to beat the cream for 3–4 minutes until light and
fluffy. Spoon the cream generously over the sponge fingers.

Drizzle the remaining lemon curd over the top of the cream,
then scatter over the pistachios. Refrigerate before serving.

EASY TIP

The lemon curd drizzle and sponge fingers can be made up to a day in advance. Simply assemble the tiramisu on the day you will be eating it.

BLOOD ORANGE PANCAKES WITH YOGURT, MAPLE AND CINNAMON

SERVES 4

For the pancakes

100g (¾ cup) plain (all-purpose)
    flour

pinch of sea salt

200ml (scant 1 cup) sweetened
    soya or oat milk, chilled

4 tbsp sunflower oil, for frying

For the topping

2 unwaxed blood oranges, peeled
    and segmented

4 tbsp maple syrup

pinch of ground cinnamon

½ sprig of thyme, leaves picked

4 tbsp vegan Greek yogurt

If you love an elegant crêpe-style pancake, then this is the recipe for you. Hot, thin pancakes are topped with juicy blood oranges that have been simmered with maple syrup, cinnamon and thyme. Top with a little vegan Greek yogurt for creaminess and tang.

In a large bowl, whisk the flour, sea salt and milk until smooth, then refrigerate for a couple of hours.

To make the topping, add the blood orange segments to a pan, lightly pressing them with a wooden spoon to release the juices. Stir in the maple syrup, cinnamon and thyme, then simmer over a low-medium heat for 10 minutes until gently bubbling.

When you are ready to cook the pancakes, heat 1 tablespoon of the oil in a flat frying pan over a medium-high heat. Ladle in enough pancake batter to cover the base of the pan, then cook for 2–3 minutes before flipping and cooking for another 2–3 minutes until golden.

Repeat until you have 4 pancakes. Keep warm.

Lay out the pancakes on individual plates, then generously spoon over the sticky orange topping. Finish with a tablespoon of vegan yogurt.

EASY TIP

Rest the pancake mix for a couple of hours, or overnight. If leaving overnight, simply loosen with a little extra soya milk before pouring into the hot pan.

SUMMER FRUIT TRAYCAKE ❄

MAKES ABOUT 8 SQUARES

250g (2 cups) self-raising flour

100g (½ cup) caster (superfine) sugar

½ tsp baking powder

4 strawberries, hulled and quartered

4 raspberries, quartered

1 tbsp blueberries, halved

250ml (1 cup) sweetened soya milk

100ml (scant ½ cup) sunflower oil

1 tsp good-quality vanilla extract

zest and juice of ½ unwaxed lemon

For the drizzle

zest and juice of ½ unwaxed lemon

150g (1½ cups) icing (confectioner's) sugar

It's always good to have a go-to traycake recipe, and this one is light and zesty, as well as being very easy to bake. Serve with a cup of tea or wrap in greaseproof paper or cling film (plastic wrap) for a packed-lunch treat.

Preheat the oven to 180°C/350°F/gas mark 4. Line a small rectangular cake tin (30 x 20cm/12 x 8in) with baking parchment.

In a large bowl, stir together the flour, sugar, baking powder, strawberries, raspberries and blueberries.

In a jug (pitcher), whisk together the soya milk, sunflower oil, vanilla extract, lemon zest and juice. Fold the liquid mixture into the dry mixture until just combined.

Pour into the prepared cake tin, then bake in the oven for 20–25 minutes until lightly golden and risen.

Meanwhile, prepare the drizzle. In a small bowl, mix together the lemon zest and juice and the icing sugar until smooth. Set aside at room temperature.

Remove the traycake from the oven and allow to cool for a few minutes. Spoon over the lemon drizzle, then serve.

EASY TIP

I love the addition of strawberries, raspberries and blueberries, but feel free to switch up for the seasons! Blackberries and figs are delicious in the autumn, or sliced plums and pears in the winter.

PAST

A

PASTA E CECI

SERVES 4

1 tbsp olive oil

1 onion, finely diced

1 garlic clove, crushed

pinch of chilli (red pepper) flakes

1 x 400g (14oz) jar or can of
    chickpeas, drained and rinsed

1 litre (4 cups) hot vegetable stock

2 tsp tomato purée (paste)

120g (4oz) dried margheritine or
    macaroni pasta (ensure vegan)

2 sprigs of fresh rosemary

generous pinch of sea salt and
    black pepper

This is one of the most comforting and underrated soups, and one that I love to make on a Sunday ready for simple lunches for the start of the week. Chickpeas and pasta are simmered with rosemary, vegetable stock and plenty of black pepper. Like so many soups, the flavour improves when made the day before – simply add a splash of water before reheating to loosen and refresh.

Heat the oil in a large pan over a low-medium heat and add the onion, garlic and chilli flakes. Cook gently for 4–5 minutes until fragrant and starting to become translucent.

Stir in the chickpeas, vegetable stock and tomato purée, followed by the pasta and rosemary.

Bring to the boil over a high heat, then reduce the heat and simmer for 20–25 minutes.

Remove from the heat and discard the rosemary sprigs. Add about a quarter of the mix (4 ladles) to a high-powered blender and blitz on high until smooth.

Pour this back into the pan and gently reheat as you stir to combine with the rest of the soup. Season with salt and plenty of black pepper.

EASY TIP

Don't miss out the step of blending some of the soup: it creates a silky, comforting texture and thickens the soup beautifully.

PANTRY MINESTRONE ❄

SERVES 4 GENEROUSLY

1 tbsp olive oil

1 onion, diced

1 celery stick, diced

2 carrots, peeled and chopped
   into half rounds

1 tsp dried oregano

500g (2 cups) good-quality
   passata (sieved tomatoes)

500ml (2 cups) hot vegetable
   stock

4 tbsp dried small soup pasta
   (ensure vegan)

2 tbsp frozen or fresh podded
   broad (fava) beans

generous pinch of sea salt and
   black pepper

small handful of flat-leaf parsley,
   finely chopped

A great minestrone recipe is at the heart of family cooking. This hearty, brothy soup makes the perfect lunch or light supper that warms the body and soul. Freeze a few portions for when you need a comforting bowl of soup, without any effort.

Add the oil, onion, celery, carrots and oregano to a large pan and cook for 5–6 minutes over a low-medium heat until the onion begins to soften but not brown.

Pour in the passata and vegetable stock, then add the pasta. Bring to the boil, then simmer over a medium heat for 30 minutes, stirring frequently to stop the pasta sticking to the pan.

Add the broad beans and cook for a further 5 minutes.

Remove from the heat and season to taste with salt and plenty of pepper. Scatter with parsley before serving.

EASY TIP

Choose your favourite small pasta for this minestrone. My favourites are dried margheritine and orzo – or even broken spaghetti!

GREEK-STYLE ORZO SALAD WITH TZATZIKI

SERVES 2 GENEROUSLY

200g (7oz) dried orzo pasta
(ensure vegan)

10 pitted black olives, thinly sliced

½ red onion, finely diced

10 cherry tomatoes, quartered

4 sundried tomatoes in oil, drained
and roughly chopped

1 tbsp flaked (slivered) almonds

juice of ½ unwaxed lemon

For the tzatziki

4 rounded tbsp vegan
Greek-style yogurt

handful of flat-leaf parsley,
finely chopped

small handful of dill,
finely chopped

5cm (2in) piece of cucumber

drizzle of extra virgin olive oil

generous pinch of sea salt and
black pepper

Serve this salad as a main meal on a warm summer's day, or pack into a lunchbox. Rice-shaped orzo pasta is quick to cook, filling and holds up to the creamy tzatziki dressing. Vegan Greek-style yogurt is available in most supermarkets, and has a thicker, creamier texture than standard vegan yogurt.

Bring a pan of water to the boil over a high heat, then add the orzo. Cook for 8–10 minutes until al dente, then drain thoroughly. Allow to cool for a few minutes before tipping into a large bowl.

Stir in the olives, red onion, cherry tomatoes, sundried tomatoes and flaked almonds. Add the lemon juice and stir to combine. Set aside to infuse.

In another bowl, stir together the vegan yogurt, parsley and dill and season with salt and pepper.

Grate the cucumber into a sieve, then use the back of a spoon to push out as much of the liquid as possible. Stir the grated cucumber into the yogurt mix, then drizzle with a little extra virgin olive oil.

Spoon the tzatziki into the orzo salad and stir through to coat.

EASY TIP

To make the salad go further, or for an extra protein boost, add a 400g (14oz) jar or can of chickpeas that have been drained and rinsed, then spoon in an additional tablespoon of vegan Greek-style yogurt.

ROASTED BUTTERNUT SQUASH AND CHESTNUT MUSHROOM TAGLIATELLE WITH SAGE

SERVES 4

½ butternut squash, skin on but scrubbed clean, chopped into bite-sized pieces

1 red onion, quartered

2 garlic cloves, peeled but left whole

1 tsp dried sage

generous drizzle of olive oil, plus extra to finish

8 chestnut (cremini) mushrooms, brushed clean, halved

8 nests of dried tagliatelle (ensure vegan)

2 rounded tbsp vegan crème fraîche

generous pinch of sea salt and black pepper

I love this cosy pasta served on a rainy autumn evening. Golden, herby and warming, with ribbons of tagliatelle to hold the smooth sauce. Add an extra nest of pasta per person if you're particularly hungry.

Preheat the oven to 180°C/350°F/gas mark 4.

Arrange the butternut squash and onion in a large roasting tray and tuck the garlic under pieces of butternut squash (to stop it from burning). Scatter with the sage, then drizzle with olive oil. Roast in the oven for 20 minutes.

Carefully remove the tray from the oven and add the halved mushrooms. Return the tray to the oven and roast for a further 10–12 minutes until the vegetables have softened.

Meanwhile, bring a large pan of salted water to the boil and add the tagliatelle. Cook for 8–10 minutes until al dente, then drain away the water.

Carefully spoon around half of the roasted butternut squash, into the jug of a high-powered blender, along with all of the onion and garlic. Add the vegan crème fraîche and 100ml (scant ½ cup) hot water, then blitz on high until completely smooth. Season with salt and pepper to taste.

Stir the sauce through the cooked tagliatelle, then stir in the remaining chunks of butternut squash and the mushrooms.

Serve in shallow bowls, with an extra pinch of salt and plenty of pepper. Drizzle over a little extra olive oil, if you like.

EASY TIP

Use the remaining uncooked half of the butternut squash to make autumn roasting-pan soup (page 127).

LOW AND SLOW LENTIL RAGÙ WITH PAPPARDELLE ❄

SERVES 4

1 tbsp olive oil, plus extra for drizzling

1 onion, diced

2 carrots, diced

2 celery sticks, diced

3 garlic cloves, crushed

1 sprig of thyme, leaves picked

1 tsp dried oregano

generous glug of red wine (ensure vegan)

1 x 400g (14oz) can of good-quality chopped tomatoes

2 tbsp tomato purée (paste)

1 x 400g (14oz) can of cooked Puy (French) lentils (or use a pouch), drained and rinsed

2 bay leaves

500g (1lb 2oz) dried pappardelle (ensure vegan)

generous pinch of sea salt and black pepper

handful of small basil leaves, to serve

Cook this on a slow afternoon when you've got nowhere to go except to potter in and out of the kitchen to stir this rich ragù. Pappardelle is a thick ribbon pasta, that holds the slow-cooked ragù perfectly, but tagliatelle is a good alternative (I've even used spaghetti here too).

In a large pan, add the oil, onion, carrots and celery and cook gently over a medium heat for 4–5 minutes until the onion begins to soften.

Add the garlic, thyme and oregano and cook for 2 minutes, then pour in the red wine and reduce for 5 minutes.

Stir in the chopped tomatoes, tomato purée and Puy lentils, along with 100ml (scant ½ cup) cold water. Lay in the bay leaves, then bring to a simmer over a medium heat. Once simmering, reduce the heat to low and cook for 1 hour, stirring frequently. If the mix becomes too dry, add another splash of water.

To cook the pappardelle, bring a large pan of salted water to the boil, then add the pasta. Cook for 8–10 minutes until al dente, then drain.

Remove the ragù from the heat and discard the bay leaves. Season generously with salt and pepper.

Tip the cooked pappardelle into the pan of ragù and stir to coat. Scatter with basil leaves just before serving and add an extra drizzle of olive oil, if you like.

EASY TIP

Puy lentils give an unmistakable depth of colour and earthy flavour to the ragù. Green lentils are a good alternative, but consider adding 1 teaspoon yeast extract when simmering, to pack in the savoury flavour.

CAULIFLOWER MAC AND CHEESE

SERVES 4

200g (7oz) dried macaroni
(ensure vegan)

1 small cauliflower, broken into
small florets, leaves discarded

50g (2oz) vegan butter

50g (2oz) plain (all-purpose) flour

500ml (2 cups) unsweetened soya
or oat milk

200g (7oz) cheddar-style vegan
hard cheese, grated

generous pinch of sea salt and
black pepper

small handful of chives,
finely chopped

Combine the home-cooked classics of cauliflower cheese and macaroni cheese in this comforting bake, perfect for family suppers. Scatter the golden and bubbling bake with chives, or grate over a little nutmeg for extra comfort.

Preheat the oven to 190°C/375°F/gas mark 5.

Bring a pan of water to the boil and add the macaroni. Cook for 8 minutes until al dente, adding the cauliflower for the final 4–5 minutes of cooking. Drain thoroughly.

Meanwhile, prepare the cheese sauce. Add the butter to another pan and gently melt over a low heat. Stir in the flour and keep stirring until a thick paste (roux) is created. Cook for a further 2 minutes.

Using a balloon whisk, gradually pour in the milk, whisking as you go. If the mixture appears to separate or split, whisk until it comes together before adding any more milk. Once all of the milk is added, whisk continuously for 10 minutes, keeping the pan on the heat, until it becomes a thick, smooth sauce. Remove from the heat and fold in most of the grated cheese, saving a generous handful for later. Season with plenty of salt and pepper.

Stir in the macaroni and cauliflower until coated in the sauce, then pour all of the mixture into a deep ovenproof dish. Scatter the remaining cheese over the top.

Bake in the oven for 45–50 minutes until the top is golden and bubbling. Remove from the oven and scatter with chives, then serve hot.

EASY TIP

Many brands of cheddar-style vegan cheese are available in supermarkets, so choose your favourite when it comes to strength and maturity. The slight tang of the cheddar flavour is delicious in the smooth white sauce.

MEDITERRANEAN BAKED ORZO WITH LEMON AND BASIL

SERVES 4

1 courgette (zucchini), chopped into half rounds

1 aubergine (eggplant), diced

1 red onion, quartered

6 cherry tomatoes

generous drizzle of olive oil

1 tsp dried oregano

1 tbsp Dijon mustard

1 garlic clove, crushed

600ml (2½ cups) hot vegetable stock

300g (10oz) dried orzo (ensure vegan)

juice of 1 unwaxed lemon

pinch of sea salt and black pepper

generous handful of basil leaves, roughly torn

Orzo becomes creamy and comforting when baked, making it the perfect pasta for this dish. This simple, effortless supper is a weeknight staple in my kitchen. Perfect for eating from a bowl with a spoon or serving with a peppery rocket (arugula) salad on the side.

Preheat the oven to 180°C/350°F/gas mark 4.

Arrange the courgette, aubergine, red onion and tomatoes in a large deep roasting tray and drizzle with olive oil. Scatter over the oregano and then roast in the oven for 20–25 minutes.

Meanwhile, stir the mustard and garlic into a jug (pitcher) of the hot vegetable stock.

Remove the roasting tray from the oven and pour in the orzo and the vegetable-stock mix. If the tray appears too small for these additional ingredients, transfer the roasted vegetables to a deep cast-iron or heatproof glass dish, then add the orzo and stock mix. Bake for a further 20 minutes.

Remove from the oven and leave to stand for about 5 minutes to absorb any excess stock. Stir in the lemon juice and season to taste with salt and plenty of pepper.

Scatter with basil just before serving.

_____

EASY TIP

For an easy variation, switch the Dijon mustard for a tablespoon of tomato purée (paste).

EASIEST-EVER WEEKNIGHT TOMATO AND CHILLI PENNE

SERVES 2

1 tbsp olive oil

2 garlic cloves, crushed

generous pinch of chilli (red pepper) flakes

400g (14oz) good-quality passata (sieved tomatoes)

½ tsp granulated sugar

150g (5oz) dried penne pasta (ensure vegan)

generous pinch of sea salt and black pepper

small handful of flat-leaf parsley, finely chopped

Sometimes, you just need an effortless bowl of pasta for supper, which is ready in less than 15 minutes. I love the way the sauce sits in the penne 'tubes', but it also works well with fusilli, conchiglie and farfalle.

Add the oil, garlic and chilli flakes to a pan and place over a medium heat for 2–3 minutes until fragrant and softened (take care not to brown the garlic).

Stir in the passata and sugar, then simmer for 10 minutes, stirring frequently.

Meanwhile bring a large pan of salted water to the boil and add the penne. Cook for 8–10 minutes until al dente, then drain.

Season the sauce with salt and pepper, then add the cooked penne and stir to coat. Serve in deep bowls, scattered with the chopped parsley.

EASY TIP

This sauce will last in the fridge for up to 3 days; it can also be frozen for up to 3 months.

AUBERGINE LASAGNE AL FORNO

SERVES 4 GENEROUSLY

For the cheese sauce

50g (2oz) vegan butter

50g (2oz) plain (all-purpose) flour

500ml (2 cups) unsweetened soya or oat milk

100g (3½oz) vegan hard cheese, grated

generous pinch of sea salt and black pepper

For the tomato sauce

1 tbsp olive oil

1 onion, diced

3 garlic cloves, crushed

1 x 400g (14oz) can of good-quality chopped tomatoes

pinch of granulated sugar

sprig of rosemary

generous pinch of sea salt and black pepper

To assemble

8 dried lasagne sheets (ensure vegan)

1 large aubergine (eggplant), thinly sliced lengthways

This vegan hybrid of two classic Italian dishes – aubergine parmigiana and lasagne – is tasty and filling, perfect for serving al fresco with a green salad and a slice of garlic bread. I love to use my favourite mature cheddar-style vegan cheese, but smoked vegan cheese makes for a deliciously unexpected twist.

For the cheese sauce, melt the vegan butter in a pan over a low heat, then use a balloon whisk to mix in the flour. Cook and whisk for 2 minutes until a paste (roux) forms. Gradually whisk in the milk, stirring continuously for 10 minutes until it becomes a thick, smooth sauce. Stir in most of the cheese, reserving a handful for topping later, and season with salt and pepper.

Preheat the oven to 180°C/350°F/gas mark 4.

Make the tomato sauce by heating the oil and onion in a pan over a medium heat for 4–5 minutes until softened but not browned, then add the garlic and cook for a further minute. Pour in the chopped tomatoes and sugar, then add the rosemary sprig. Simmer for 15 minutes, then discard the rosemary. Season to taste with plenty of salt and pepper.

Take a large, rectangular lasagne dish and add lasagne sheets to cover the base of the dish, then spoon a thin layer of tomato sauce over the top. Lay thin slices of aubergine to cover the tomato sauce, then smooth over a layer of cheese sauce. Repeat with even layers until you reach the top of the dish.

Place the dish onto a baking tray and scatter the top with the remaining grated cheese. Cook in the oven for 1 hour until bubbling and golden.

EASY TIP

There's no need to pre-cook the lasagne sheets, as they will soften with the moisture from the tomato sauce during the cooking time.

SPEEDY LEMON, CHILLI AND PEA FARFALLE

SERVES 2

200g (7oz) (or more if you're hungry) dried farfalle pasta (ensure vegan)

2 tbsp frozen peas

generous handful of baby spinach leaves, stems discarded

2 tbsp good-quality extra virgin olive oil, plus extra for drizzling

2 garlic cloves, crushed

generous pinch of chilli (red pepper) flakes

juice of 1 large unwaxed lemon

generous pinch of sea salt and black pepper

small handful of flat-leaf parsley, finely chopped

Sometimes you just need an easy, fresh supper that is ready in less than 15 minutes. I love to use this butterfly-shaped pasta, not only because it's pretty, but it fits perfectly onto a spoon, making it the ideal pasta for a low-effort supper. The leftovers are great for packed lunches the following day, served hot or cold.

Bring a large pan of salted water to the boil, then add the pasta. Simmer for 8 minutes, then add the peas and spinach and cook for a further minute. Drain through a sieve or colander and set aside.

Return the empty pan to the hob and add the olive oil, garlic and chilli flakes. Cook over a low heat for 3–4 minutes until fragrant and softened.

Add the cooked pasta, peas and spinach back into the pan and stir through the fragrant oil. Pour in the lemon juice and stir through to distribute evenly.

Season with salt and plenty of pepper. Drizzle with a little more extra virgin olive oil, if you like, then scatter over the parsley just before serving.

EASY TIP

If you prefer your lemon pasta on the creamy side, stir in 2 tablespoons vegan crème fraîche with the lemon juice before warming through.

COCO
MILK

NUT

AUTUMN ROASTING-PAN SOUP ❄

SERVES 4

½ butternut squash, skin on, chopped into even 2cm (¾in) chunks

1 large sweet potato, peeled and chopped into 2cm (¾in) chunks

1 leek, roughly chopped

1 carrot, peeled and roughly chopped

1 tsp dried sage

drizzle of sunflower oil

1 x 400ml (14fl oz) can of full-fat coconut milk

400ml (generous 1¾ cups) hot vegetable stock

generous pinch of sea salt and black pepper

toasted oat topper (page 16), to serve (optional)

While your Sunday roast is cooking in the oven, throw in this roasting tray full of seasonal vegetables, ready for blitzing into a warming soup for lunches through the week. Coconut milk gives this soup a creamy, silky texture without taking away from the flavoursome sage and root vegetables.

Preheat the oven to 180°C/350°F/gas mark 4.

Arrange the squash, sweet potato, leek and carrot in a large roasting tray and sprinkle over the sage.

Drizzle with sunflower oil, then roast in the oven for 30 minutes until the vegetables have softened and some of the edges are crisp.

Spoon into the jug of a high-powered blender and pour in the coconut milk and half of the vegetable stock. Blitz until completely smooth, adding more stock as you go to reach your preferred thickness and texture.

Season to taste with salt and plenty of black pepper. Serve in warmed bowls and top with the toasted oat topper on page 16, if you like.

EASY TIP

There's no need to peel the skin off the butternut squash; simply give it a good scrub clean before roasting and pack in that extra nutrition and flavour.

EASY CREAMY NOODLES

SERVES 2

1 x 400ml (14fl oz) can of full-fat
    coconut milk

2 tsp Thai red curry paste
    (ensure vegan)

pinch of chilli (red pepper) flakes

4 stems of Tenderstem broccoli
    (broccolini), trimmed

4 sugarsnap (snap) peas,
    sliced lengthways

1 carrot, peeled and grated

2 tsp dark soy sauce

300g (10oz) soft straight-to-wok
    noodles (ensure vegan)

handful of coriander (cilantro),
    roughly torn

juice of ½ unwaxed lime

2 spring onions (scallions),
    finely chopped

1 red chilli, sliced (optional)

**Simmer up a bowlful of these creamy noodles for lunch,
whether you're eating at home or reheating at the office.
Stir in a tablespoon of frozen edamame beans, or scatter
over a handful of peanuts for extra protein, if you like.**

Pour the coconut milk into a pan and stir in the curry paste
and chilli flakes. Bring to a simmer over a medium-high heat.

Add the broccoli, sugarsnap peas and grated carrot, then
simmer for 5–6 minutes until the broccoli is tender and bright
in colour.

Stir in the soy sauce, then add the noodles and cook for
3–4 minutes until hot.

Remove from the heat and stir in the coriander and lime juice.
Scatter over the spring onions and red chilli (if using) and
serve hot.

EASY TIP

You'll find egg-free soft noodles in the ambient aisles of
supermarkets – the chilled soft noodles kept in the fridges
are more likely to contain eggs. Always check the ingredients
before you buy. If the noodles feel a little starchy in the packet,
simply rinse them in hot water through a sieve.

FLUFFY COCONUT RICE ❄

SERVES 4 AS A SIDE DISH

4 tbsp desiccated (dried shredded) coconut

350g (generous 1½ cups) jasmine rice, rinsed in cold water

1 x 400ml (14fl oz) can of full-fat coconut milk

pinch of sea salt

When you need a tasty yet simple side dish, this coconut rice is packed with flavour. It is delicious served with gochujang sticky no-meatballs (page 21) or to soak up the spices from comforting leeks and lentils with lemon and ginger (page 69).

Add the coconut to a large dry pan and toast over a high heat for 2–3 minutes until golden. Set aside in a bowl.

Add the rinsed rice to the pan, along with the coconut milk and 250ml (1 cup) cold water. Place a lid loosely over the pan. Bring to the boil over a high heat, then reduce the heat and simmer for 15 minutes.

Remove from the heat and place the lid securely on the pan. Allow to stand for 10 minutes.

Stir in the sea salt and toasted desiccated coconut, then use a fork to fluff up the rice.

EASY TIP

Jasmine rice soaks up the flavour and creaminess of the coconut milk really well and becomes fluffy without clumping. Basmati is a good alternative if you don't have jasmine rice.

GINGER BRAISED MUSHROOMS WITH COCONUT

SERVES 4

1 tbsp sunflower oil

3cm (1¼in) piece of ginger, grated

200g (7oz) pack of mixed and exotic mushrooms, brushed clean, roughly sliced or chopped

200g (7oz) chestnut (cremini) mushrooms, brushed clean, roughly sliced or chopped

2 garlic cloves, crushed

1 tbsp dark soy sauce

1 x 400ml (14fl oz) can of full-fat coconut milk

2 tsp Thai green curry paste (ensure vegan)

handful of flat-leaf parsley, finely chopped

1 small red chilli, deseeded and finely sliced

2 spring onions (scallions), finely chopped

generous pinch of black pepper

This is one of my favourite ways to eat mushrooms: braised with fresh ginger, garlic and dark soy sauce to celebrate their earthy, unique flavour. Serve in bowls or deep dishes with the creamy spiced coconut sauce, with plenty of fresh chilli and black pepper.

Add the oil, ginger and mushrooms to a wok and cook over a medium heat for 8–10 minutes until softened. Stir in the garlic and soy sauce and cook until for 2 minutes until fragrant.

Meanwhile, add the coconut milk and Thai green curry paste to a pan and bring to the boil over a medium heat. Simmer for 10 minutes until combined and slightly reduced, then remove from the heat and stir in the parsley.

Ladle the hot, spiced coconut milk into bowls, then spoon on the mushrooms. Scatter with chilli and spring onions and finish with plenty of black pepper.

EASY TIP

You'll find small boxes of mixed and exotic mushrooms at large supermarkets. This is a great way to try new mushrooms; alternatively, pick up individual packs of your favourites.

OVEN-BAKED
BUTTER CHICKPEAS ❄

SERVES 4

1 small cauliflower, torn into
  bite-sized florets, leaves
  and stem discarded

8 new or baby potatoes

1 red onion, quartered

drizzle of sunflower oil

1 x 400ml (14fl oz) can of full-fat
  coconut milk

1 tbsp medium curry paste

1 tbsp tomato purée (paste)

1 tbsp mango chutney

pinch of chilli (red pepper) flakes

1 tbsp sultanas (golden raisins)

1 x 400g (14oz) can or jar of
  chickpeas, drained and rinsed

generous pinch of sea salt

juice of ½ unwaxed lemon

small handful of coriander
  (cilantro) leaves, to serve

Coconut milk is the perfect alternative to dairy butter and cream in this recipe, as when oven-baked, its flavour is intensified, becoming creamier and gently sweeter. Combine this with mango chutney, spices, chickpeas and twice-roasted vegetables for a comforting supper that lets the oven do all of the hard work. Serve with pilau rice, or a vegan naan bread for dipping.

Preheat the oven to 200°C/400°F/gas mark 6.

Arrange the cauliflower, potatoes and red onion in a large, deep roasting tray, or over two smaller trays. Drizzle with sunflower oil, then roast in the oven for 20 minutes.

Meanwhile, pour the coconut milk into a jug (pitcher) or bowl, then whisk in the curry paste, tomato purée, mango chutney and chilli flakes. Set aside.

Carefully remove the roasting tray from the oven and add the sultanas and chickpeas. Pour the spiced coconut milk around the vegetables, fully coating the sultanas and chickpeas.

Return the roasting tray to the oven and cook for 30 minutes until the simmering sauce has thickened and the vegetables have softened.

Remove from the oven and season with salt. Drizzle over the lemon juice and scatter with coriander leaves just before serving.

EASY TIP

Use a deep roasting tray that will hold all of the ingredients, plus the coconut sauce. If your roasting tray appears too full, transfer the ingredients to a cast-iron or ovenproof glass casserole dish.

ROASTED DIPPING POTATOES WITH SMOKED PEPPER SAUCE

SERVES 4

2 tbsp olive oil

3 garlic cloves

2 tsp smoked paprika

pinch of chilli (red pepper) flakes

200g (7oz) jar of chargrilled red (bell) peppers in oil, drained

4 sundried tomatoes in oil from a jar, drained

1 tbsp tomato purée (paste)

1 x 400ml (14fl oz) can of full-fat coconut milk

800g (1lb 12oz) new potatoes

1 tbsp sherry vinegar

generous pinch of sea salt and black pepper

½ small red onion, finely diced

small handful of flat-leaf parsley, finely chopped

Serve these perfectly roasted potatoes as a sharing dish, for family and friends to dip into the twice-cooked smoked sauce. Or enjoy them as a tasty supper, with a handful of toasted pine nuts or flaked almonds, with a side of butterbeans (lima beans) drizzled in lemon juice.

Add 1 tablespoon of the oil to a large pan with the garlic, smoked paprika and chilli flakes. Soften over a medium-high heat for 2 minutes, then stir in the peppers, sundried tomatoes and tomato purée. Pour in the coconut milk and bring to the boil, then reduce the heat and simmer for 15–20 minutes.

Preheat the oven to 180°C/350°F/gas mark 4.

Arrange the new potatoes in a large, deep roasting tray or dish and drizzle with the remaining tablespoon of oil. Roast in the oven for 20 minutes.

Meanwhile, remove the pan from the hob and carefully pour or ladle the contents into a high-powered blender jug. Add the sherry vinegar, then blitz until completely smooth.

Remove the roasting dish from the oven and pour the smooth pepper sauce around the potatoes, avoiding the tops where you can. Return the dish to the oven for a further 20 minutes, until the tops of the potatoes are golden brown and the sauce has thickened further.

Remove from the oven and season with salt and pepper. Scatter over the red onion and parsley just before serving.

EASY TIP

You'll find jars of chargrilled red peppers in supermarkets and delis; they are perfect for packing flavour into this sauce, as well as topping pizzas or enjoying as part of mezze.

COCONUT, MANGO
AND LIME MARINADE ❄

SERVES 4

1 x 400ml (14fl oz) can of full-fat
  coconut milk

1 very ripe mango, peeled and
  stone discarded

2cm (¾in) piece of ginger, grated

zest and juice of 1 unwaxed lime

1 tsp chilli (red pepper) flakes

1 tsp smoked sea salt

**Every home cook needs a great marinade recipe that is easy
to whip up, ready to flavour tofu, tempeh and vegetables
such as sweet potatoes, aubergine (eggplant) and courgettes
(zucchini). Follow by roasting, grilling or barbecuing – or
simply pan-fry your way to a delicious supper. Use this
marinade to coat your favourite ingredients in a glass bowl,
container or ziplock bag, always for at least one hour.**

Add the coconut milk, mango, ginger, lime zest and juice to a
high-powered blender jug and blitz until thick and smooth.

Stir in the chilli flakes and smoked sea salt. Use straight away or
freeze to use another time.

_____

EASY TIP

Freeze this marinade in two batches so you always
have the perfect quantity ready to defrost and use.

CHARRED VEGETABLE THAI-STYLE RED CURRY ❄

SERVES 4 GENEROUSLY

2 tbsp sunflower oil

3cm (1¼in) piece of ginger, grated

3 garlic cloves, crushed

½ tsp chilli (red pepper) flakes

1 rounded tbsp Thai red curry paste (ensure vegan)

1 x 400ml (14fl oz) can of full-fat coconut milk

2 tsp smooth peanut butter

1 red (bell) pepper, sliced into chunks

8 sugarsnap (snap) peas

8 baby corns, halved

8 chunks of pineapple (canned or fresh)

2 spring onions (scallions), finely chopped

2 tsp dark soy sauce

handful of salted peanuts, roughly chopped

small handful of Thai basil leaves

Whip up this creamy, perfectly spiced curry with charred vegetables in 30 minutes. Thai basil is available in some large supermarkets and has a deeper, more liquorice flavour than regular basil, with a kick of fresh spice. If you can't source Thai basil, use a handful of regular basil with a few small mint leaves and plenty of fresh coriander (cilantro).

Add 1 tablespoon of the oil to a large pan and throw in the ginger, garlic and chilli flakes. Cook over a low-medium heat for 3-4 minutes until softened and fragrant.

Stir in the Thai red curry paste and coconut milk, followed by the peanut butter. Bring to a gentle boil over a high heat, then reduce the heat and simmer for 20 minutes, stirring frequently.

Heat a griddle (grill) pan over a medium heat while you thread the pepper chunks, sugarsnap peas, baby corns and pineapple onto metal or soaked wooden skewers. Brush with the remaining tablespoon of oil.

Place the vegetable skewers into the griddle pan and cook for 4-5 minutes, turning the skewers when char lines appear and the cooked side appears softened.

Stir the spring onions and soy sauce into the curry base. Ladle into serving bowls, then remove the vegetables from the skewers and place them on top of the curry. Scatter with peanuts and Thai basil leaves just before serving.

EASY TIP

Use metal or soaked wooden skewers to turn the vegetables easily in one go. If you don't have these available, you can add the vegetables straight onto the griddle pan, although turning them will take a little more effort and precision.

COCONUT BANOFFEE PIE

SERVES 4-6

**For the whipped coconut
 cream topping**

2 x 400ml (14fl oz) cans of full-fat
 coconut milk

For the base

200g (7oz) digestive biscuits
 (graham crackers); ensure vegan

100g (3½oz) vegan butter

For the caramel-banana centre

120g (½ cup) soft light
 brown sugar

120g (4oz) vegan butter

1 x 370g (13oz) can of vegan
 condensed milk (see easy
 tip, opposite)

1 tsp vanilla extract

2 bananas, sliced

1 tsp toasted flaked coconut

2 squares vegan dark chocolate,
 finely chopped

**This much-loved, classic recipe gets a flavour twist with
whipped coconut cream – banana, coconut and caramel are a
match made in dessert heaven! To make the whipped coconut
cream, the cans of coconut milk must be kept in the fridge
for at least 4 hours (overnight is best) so that the cream
separates from the water. I love to serve banoffee pie in a
glass bowl, to show off the layers, but feel free to make it in
a loose-bottomed tin.**

Place the unopened cans of coconut milk in the fridge for at
least 4 hours, or overnight.

Blitz the digestive biscuits in a food processor or high-powered
blender, or place in a ziplock bag and break up with a rolling pin
until the biscuits are reduced to a fine crumb.

Melt the butter in a pan over a low heat, then stir in the biscuit
crumbs until evenly combined. Press this mixture into a 20cm
(8in) glass bowl or loose-bottomed cake tin that has been lined
with baking parchment. Chill in the fridge for 30 minutes.

Meanwhile, make the caramel. Melt the brown sugar and butter
in a pan over a low heat, stirring frequently until combined.
Pour in the vegan condensed milk and vanilla extract, then
bring to a lively simmer over a medium heat. Reduce the heat
to a gentle simmer and cook for 10 minutes until the mixture
starts to thicken. Remove from the heat and allow to thicken as
it cools for 10 minutes. The mixture should coat the back of a
wooden spoon.

Pour the slightly cooled sauce over the biscuit base, then
arrange the sliced bananas over the top. Return to the fridge
for 2-3 hours.

Open the chilled cans of coconut milk and scoop the solid
coconut cream out into a bowl (save the liquid to add to a
smoothie or curry). Use a hand-held electric whisk to whip the
cream until airy with soft peaks.

Generously smooth the whipped coconut cream over the
caramel and bananas, then scatter with the toasted flaked
coconut and dark chocolate. Chill until ready to serve.

EASY TIP

You'll find vegan condensed milk in many large supermarkets, from big-brand suppliers to smaller producers. Some are made from coconut milk, while others are made from oat milk – they both work well in this recipe.

EASY PISTACHIO, MANGO AND COCONUT KULFI ❄

MAKES 4–6

100g (3½oz) shelled pistachios

1 x 400ml (14fl oz) can of full-fat coconut milk

3 tbsp soft light brown sugar

generous pinch of ground cardamom

small pinch of saffron strands

1 large ripe mango, peeled and chopped into chunks

200ml (scant 1 cup) vegan double (heavy) cream

Kulfi is a traditional Indian no-churn ice cream, usually frozen into moulds like ice lollies. Kulfi recipes are often complicated and lengthy, but I love it so much that I was determined to create a simpler, vegan version, which pays homage to this beautiful, frozen treat.

Put the pistachios into a bowl and cover with boiling water. Allow to stand for 30 minutes until softened, then drain away the water.

Pour the coconut milk into a pan with the brown sugar, cardamom and saffron. Simmer over a medium heat until the sugar has dissolved, then set aside for a few minutes to cool.

Add the softened pistachios and mango to a high-powered blender jug and blitz until semi-smooth. Pour the coconut milk mix and vegan cream into the jug, then blitz again until combined and smooth, with just a few small particles of pistachio visible.

Pour the mix into kulfi or ice-lolly moulds (depending on the size of the moulds, this should make 4–6 servings). Freeze overnight, or for at least 6 hours.

_____

EASY TIP

Allow to stand at room temperature for a few minutes before removing from the moulds. Not only will this make removal easier, but it helps to soften the first bite of this creamy iced dessert.

JACK

FRUIT

GOLDEN RICE WITH JACKFRUIT, LEMON AND DILL ❄

SERVES 4 GENEROUSLY

1 tbsp sunflower oil

1 onion, finely chopped

2 garlic cloves, crushed

2 tsp mild curry paste
(ensure vegan)

½ tsp ground turmeric

½ tsp ground cumin

250g (1½ cups) basmati rice

1 x 400g (14oz) can of jackfruit,
rinsed and broken into smaller
chunks and strands

1 bay leaf

8 green beans, halved

2 tbsp frozen peas

generous handful of dill,
finely chopped

juice of 1 unwaxed lemon

pinch of smoked sea salt and
black pepper

2 rounded tbsp unsweetened
vegan yogurt

pinch of smoked paprika

This golden rice takes inspiration from kedgeree, a British Raj-era breakfast dish traditionally made with smoked haddock. Serve this family-style, at the centre of the table, for a flavourful brunch or supper. Jackfruit is a fantastic replacement for haddock, with its flaky, tender texture. Be generous with the dill and lemon, as they transform the dish with zings of freshness and nostalgic aromas.

Add the oil and onion to a large pan and cook for 3–4 minutes over a medium-high heat until the onion begins to soften. Add the garlic and cook for a further minute.

Stir in the curry paste, turmeric and cumin until combined.

Add the rice and jackfruit, then pour in 600ml (2½ cups) cold water. Lay in the bay leaf, then bring to the boil over a high heat. Once bubbling, reduce the heat and simmer for 10 minutes, stirring frequently.

Add the green beans and peas, with an extra splash of water if the rice has absorbed the liquid, and cook for a further 5–6 minutes until the vegetables are hot and the rice is fluffy.

Remove from the heat and discard the bay leaf. Place a lid on the pan and allow to stand for 5 minutes.

Stir in the dill and lemon juice until combined, then season with smoked sea salt and black pepper. Spoon onto a large sharing plate, then spoon the yogurt over the top. Sprinkle a little smoked paprika over the yogurt to finish.

EASY TIP

Season with smoked sea salt if you have it, to really deliver on the traditional smoky flavours in the dish.

LUNCHBOX SPRING ROLLS WITH FIVE-SPICE

MAKES 6

1 tbsp sunflower oil, plus extra for brushing

1 carrot, sliced into ribbons using a vegetable peeler

1 red (bell) pepper, very thinly sliced

2 spring onions (scallions), finely chopped

2 radishes, thinly sliced

handful of shredded kale, tough stems discarded

1 x 400g (14oz) can of jackfruit, drained and broken into strands

1 garlic clove, crushed

2cm (¾in) piece of ginger, grated

2 tsp Chinese five-spice

2 tsp dark soy sauce

6 large tortilla wraps

1 tsp sesame seeds

Make a delicious spring roll more substantial for lunch by using a baked tortilla wrap. These giant spring rolls are packed with crunchy vegetables, meaty jackfruit, ginger and spices. Serve hot or cold, with sweet chilli sauce or extra soy sauce for dipping, if you like.

Preheat the oven to 190°C/375°F/gas mark 5 and lay out a large baking tray.

Heat the oil in a wok over a medium-high heat, then throw in the carrot, red pepper, spring onions, radishes, kale and jackfruit. Stir-fry for 3–4 minutes, then add the garlic, ginger, Chinese five-spice and soy sauce. Cook for another 3–4 minutes, stirring constantly.

Remove the wok from the heat. Lay a tortilla wrap on a clean surface and spoon 2–3 tablespoons of the jackfruit mixture into the centre in a line. Fold two of the sides inwards, then roll the side nearest to you towards the other side to create a secure, wrapped roll. Repeat for all of the wraps.

Place the wraps onto the baking tray and use a pastry brush to sweep over a little sunflower oil. Sprinkle with sesame seeds, then bake in the oven for 12–15 minutes, until golden and crisp.

EASY TIP

Switch these vegetables for any other crunchy vegetables you have available, including broccoli, sugarsnap (snap) peas, cabbage and courgettes (zucchini).

LEMON JACKFRUIT BAGUETTE WITH MAYO, CHIVES AND GHERKINS

SERVES 4

1 x 400g (14oz) can of jackfruit, drained and rinsed, broken into strands

juice of 1 unwaxed lemon

pinch of smoked sea salt

4 rounded tbsp vegan mayonnaise

1 tsp Dijon mustard

1 celery stick, very finely diced

generous handful of chives, finely chopped

1 tbsp sliced pickled gherkins

1 fresh white tiger baton

small handful of iceberg lettuce, torn

Use your can of jackfruit to make a tuna-style sandwich filling, using that classic mix of lemon juice, mayonnaise and chives. Smoked sea salt really makes a difference in this recipe, so use it instead of standard sea salt if you can. Sprinkle in a pinch of nori flakes for flavours of the sea, if you like.

Blot dry the jackfruit on kitchen paper or a clean tea towel, then place into a bowl.

Stir in the lemon juice and season with the smoked sea salt. Allow to infuse for 30 minutes.

Stir in the mayonnaise, mustard, celery, chives and gherkins.

Slice the tiger baton into two, then cut or tear down the centre. Add lettuce to each half, then generously spoon in the jackfruit mix. Enjoy straight away.

EASY TIP

Switch the baguette for two thick slices of white tiger or sourdough bread, for a doorstep sandwich!

SHAWARMA FLATBREADS WITH HOUMOUS AND GREEN CHILLI ❄

SERVES 4

1 tbsp sunflower oil

1 red onion, sliced

1 tsp soft brown sugar

3 garlic cloves, crushed

1 tsp smoked paprika

½ tsp ground cumin

pinch of ground cinnamon

1 x 400g (14oz) can of jackfruit, drained and rinsed, then broken into strands

½ red cabbage, shredded

juice of ½ unwaxed lime

handful of flat-leaf parsley, finely chopped

generous pinch of sea salt and black pepper

4 flatbreads (ensure vegan), warmed

4 tbsp houmous

½ iceberg lettuce, shredded

1 green chilli, deseeded and sliced into rounds

It's time for a fakeaway. When you're craving hot shawarma, loaded into flatbreads with crunchy red cabbage, houmous and fresh green chillies, jackfruit provides the perfect substitute for pulled meat in this quick recipe.

Heat the oil and red onion in a frying pan over a medium-high heat for 5 minutes, stirring occasionally to prevent sticking. Sprinkle in the brown sugar and cook for a further 2 minutes until it begins to caramelize.

Stir in the garlic, paprika, cumin and cinnamon and cook for a further minute.

Add the jackfruit and cabbage and stir to coat in the spices. Cook for 10 minutes, stirring frequently to avoid sticking.

Remove the pan from the heat and stir in the lime juice and parsley, then season to taste with salt and pepper.

Lay out the flatbreads on a clean surface and smooth 1 tablespoon of the houmous over each one. Add plenty of lettuce, then spoon in the jackfruit shawarma mix. Scatter with the sliced green chilli, then wrap the flatbread.

EASY TIP

Flatbreads are readily available in supermarkets, but always check the ingredients, as some contain dairy products, making them unsuitable for vegans.

ROASTED JACKFRUIT AND CAULIFLOWER TACOS WITH AVOCADO SALSA

SERVES 4

2 tsp smoked paprika

1 tsp mild chilli powder

pinch of ground cumin

pinch of dried oregano

pinch of chilli (red pepper) flakes

4 tbsp sunflower oil

1 cauliflower, leaves discarded, broken into bite-sized florets

1 x 400g (14oz) can of jackfruit, drained and rinsed, torn into shreds

1 red (bell) pepper, very thinly sliced

small handful of coriander (cilantro), torn

generous pinch of smoked sea salt

juice of ½ unwaxed lime

8 soft- or hard-shell tacos

4 tbsp vegan mayonnaise, chilled

For the avocado salsa

1 avocado, peeled and finely diced

1 small red onion, diced

1 x 198g (7oz) can of sweetcorn, drained

juice of ½ unwaxed lime

Have a fun supper on the table in half an hour with these tasty hot tacos, packed with spices, roasted cauliflower and peppers, and jackfruit. I love topping them with plenty of this avocado salsa, but they are equally delicious with traditional tomato salsa or pickled red onions.

Preheat the oven to 180°C/350°F/gas mark 4.

Mix the smoked paprika, chilli powder, cumin, oregano and chilli flakes in a large bowl, then add the oil and stir to combine. Toss the cauliflower florets and jackfruit into the bowl and turn to coat in the spiced oil.

Tip the cauliflower and jackfruit into a large roasting tray and scatter over the red pepper. Drizzle over any remaining spiced oil and then roast in the oven for 20–25 minutes until the cauliflower is gently golden and just softened.

Meanwhile, make the avocado salsa. Mix the avocado, red onion and sweetcorn in a bowl and drizzle over the lime juice. Set aside.

Remove the roasting tray from the oven and scatter over the coriander and smoked sea salt. Drizzle with the lime juice.

Load the hot cauliflower, jackfruit and peppers into the taco shells, then spoon a little vegan mayonnaise over each. Finish by adding generous spoonfuls of the avocado salsa.

EASY TIP

The hot taco filling can be roasted in advance and then reheated if you're short of time. The salsa will keep for up to 2 days when kept chilled in a sealed container.

WINTER POT ROAST WITH ROSEMARY ❄

SERVES 4

1 tbsp sunflower oil

1 onion, finely diced

2 celery sticks, diced

2 carrots, roughly sliced into half rounds

2 floury potatoes, peeled and roughly diced

2 garlic cloves, crushed

1 tsp dried sage

generous glug of red wine (ensure vegan)

1 x 400g (14oz) can of good-quality chopped tomatoes

600ml (2½ cups) hot vegetable stock

1 tbsp tomato purée (paste)

1 x 400g (14oz) can of jackfruit, drained and rinsed, roughly broken into smaller pieces

1 apple, cored and roughly sliced

2 sprigs of fresh rosemary

1 bay leaf

pinch of sea salt and black pepper

This one-pot supper is warming and comforting, perfect for those long winter evenings when all you crave is a bowl of home-cooked food. Rosemary and red wine flavour the jackfruit and seasonal vegetables wonderfully to create a rich gravy.

Heat the oil in a large, lidded casserole dish, add the onion and cook over a medium-high heat for 2–3 minutes until it starts to soften. Add the celery, carrots and potatoes and cook for another 2 minutes.

Throw in the garlic and dried sage and cook for 1 minute until the garlic becomes fragrant.

Pour in the red wine and reduce for 2–3 minutes, then stir in the chopped tomatoes, stock, tomato purée, jackfruit and apple. Add the rosemary and bay leaf, and loosely cover with the lid. Bring to the boil, then reduce the heat and leave to simmer for 40–45 minutes, stirring occasionally to avoid sticking, until the liquid has reduced slightly.

Remove from the heat and discard the rosemary sprigs and bay leaf. Season with salt and pepper before serving, with crusty bread.

EASY TIP

To make the dish stretch further, and for added protein, stir in a 400g (14oz) can or jar of drained and rinsed cannellini beans along with the jackfruit.

LOADED TWICE-BAKED POTATOES WITH STICKY BBQ JACKFRUIT ❄

SERVES 4 GENEROUSLY

4 large baking potatoes, scrubbed
    clean and dried

1 tbsp sunflower oil

1 red onion, diced

½ x 400g (14oz) can of jackfruit,
    drained and rinsed, broken into
    smaller pieces

2 rounded tbsp BBQ sauce
    (ensure vegan)

pinch of smoked sea salt

1 tbsp vegan butter

4 tbsp vegan oat-based
    crème fraîche

generous handful of chives,
    finely chopped, plus extra
    to finish

handful of hard vegan
    cheese, grated

If I had to choose a dish to cook on a rainy Saturday afternoon, it would be these twice-baked potatoes, stuffed with tangy, vegan crème fraîche, chives and sticky BBQ jackfruit. Perfect for when you have a little more time to spare, and perfect to enjoy in front of Saturday night TV!

Preheat the oven to 200°C/400°F/gas mark 6.

Bake the potatoes for 1 hour until the skin is crispy and the inside is softened and fluffy. If the potatoes are very large, cook for an extra 10–20 minutes, checking at regular intervals.

Meanwhile, add the oil, red onion and jackfruit to a pan and cook for 2–3 minutes over a medium heat until the onion begins to soften. Add the BBQ sauce and stir to coat the jackfruit, allowing it to gently bubble at the edges. Stir in the smoked sea salt and set aside.

Remove the baked potatoes from the oven and allow them to cool for a few minutes until you can handle them comfortably. Slice each potato in half, then use a spoon to scoop out the soft potato centre into a bowl.

Add the butter, crème fraîche and chives to the potato and stir to combine fully, then spoon the sticky jackfruit and red onion into the potato mixture, shaking off any excess sauce as you go.

Spoon this mixture generously back into the potato halves, then sprinkle with grated cheese.

Return to the oven and bake for 15–20 minutes, or until golden and bubbling. Sprinkle with chopped chives to finish.

EASY TIP

Freeze any uncooked leftover jackfruit – most cans are 400g (14oz), so you'll only need half a can for this recipe – or use it for masala jackfruit naan pizzas with raita (page 167).

JACKFRUIT, COCONUT AND BLACK BEANS WITH MANGO ❄

SERVES 2

1 tbsp sunflower oil

1 onion, diced

1 red (bell) pepper, roughly diced

2cm (¾in) piece of ginger, grated

2 garlic cloves, crushed

2 tsp jerk seasoning

pinch of chilli (red pepper) flakes

1 x 400ml (14fl oz) can of full-fat coconut milk

1 x 400g (14oz) can of jackfruit, drained and rinsed, broken into small pieces

1 x 400g (14oz) jar or can of black beans, drained and rinsed

handful of coriander (cilantro) leaves, chopped

1 mango, peeled and diced

generous pinch of sea salt

½ unwaxed lime, for squeezing (optional)

Close your eyes and take yourself to warmer climates, with the taste of the Caribbean in this easy one-pot that combines jackfruit and black beans with spices, coconut milk and juicy mango. Serve with rice, or a few sweet potato fries.

Add the oil, onion and pepper to a large pan over a medium heat and cook for 2–3 minutes. Stir in the ginger, garlic, jerk seasoning and chilli flakes and cook for a further 2 minutes, stirring constantly.

Pour in the coconut milk, then add the jackfruit and black beans. Bring to a gentle boil, then reduce the heat slightly and simmer for 25 minutes, stirring occasionally.

Remove from the heat and stir through the coriander and diced mango, reserving a few pieces to garnish. Season to taste with sea salt. Spoon into serving dishes, then scatter with the reserved mango. Squeeze the lime juice over the top, if using.

EASY TIP

Jerk seasoning is a pre-mixed spice blend available in most supermarkets. It has a mix of cloves, allspice, cumin, paprika and cinnamon, giving any dish a taste of the Caribbean.

SLOW-COOKED PULLED JACKFRUIT CHILLI ❄

SERVES 4 GENEROUSLY

1 tbsp sunflower oil

1 onion, diced

2 celery sticks, diced

1 yellow (bell) pepper, diced

2 garlic cloves

1 rounded tsp chilli powder

1 tsp smoked paprika

½ tsp ground cinnamon

1 sprig of thyme

1 x 400g (14oz) can of good-quality
  chopped tomatoes

1 tbsp tomato purée (paste)

1 x 400g (14oz) can of jackfruit,
  rinsed and broken into smaller
  chunks and strands

1 x 400g (14oz) can of red kidney
  beans, drained and rinsed

1 tsp yeast extract

1 tsp soft light brown sugar

juice of 1 unwaxed lime

handful of coriander (cilantro)
  leaves, roughly torn

generous pinch of smoked sea salt
  and black pepper

Give your chilli some texture with pulled jackfruit and the enticing flavours of cinnamon, smoked paprika and lime. Serve with rice, jacket potatoes or a handful of tortilla chips, as well as a side of store-cupboard salsa (page 42).

Add the oil, onion, celery and yellow pepper to a large pan and cook over a medium heat for 4–5 minutes until the onion begins to soften.

Add the garlic, chilli powder, paprika and cinnamon, then remove the leaves of the thyme sprig and stir them in. Cook for 2 minutes, stirring frequently.

Pour in the chopped tomatoes and tomato purée, then stir in the jackfruit, red kidney beans, yeast extract and brown sugar. Bring to a gentle simmer, then reduce the heat to low and place a lid loosely over the pan. Cook for 45 minutes, stirring frequently to avoid sticking.

Remove from the heat and stir through the lime juice and coriander leaves. Season to taste with smoked sea salt and black pepper.

EASY TIP

Black beans or borlotti beans make a good alternative to red kidney beans in this chilli. Use as an alternative or as an addition to make this chilli stretch further.

MASALA JACKFRUIT NAAN PIZZAS WITH RAITA

SERVES 4

½ x 400g (14oz) can of jackfruit, drained and rinsed, broken into smaller chunks

1 tbsp sunflower oil

1 garlic clove, crushed

1 rounded tsp garam masala

generous pinch of chilli (red pepper) flakes

juice from ½ unwaxed lemon

2 large garlic naan breads (ensure vegan)

4 rounded tbsp tomato purée (paste)

1 red onion, thinly sliced

4 mushrooms, sliced

1 green (bell) pepper, sliced

drizzle of olive oil

generous pinch of black pepper

small handful of coriander (cilantro), roughly torn

For the raita

4 rounded tbsp thick coconut yogurt, chilled

small handful of mint leaves, finely chopped

generous pinch of sea salt

The whole family will love these gently spiced, filling pizzas with naan bread bases. Most cans of jackfruit are around 400g (14oz), and while you can use the whole can for this recipe (if you like a generous topping), feel free to freeze the uncooked jackfruit or use for loaded twice-baked potatoes with sticky BBQ jackfruit (page 160) another day.

Preheat the oven to 180°C/350°F/gas mark 4.

Blot the rinsed jackfruit with kitchen paper or a clean tea towel. Add the sunflower oil and jackfruit to a frying pan, sprinkle in the garlic, garam masala and chilli flakes and cook for 4–5 minutes over a medium heat until fragrant. Drizzle over the lemon juice, then remove from the heat and set aside.

Lay out the naan breads on a work surface and spread over the tomato purée. Press in the red onion, mushrooms and green pepper slices, then generously spoon on the masala jackfruit.

Place on baking trays, then drizzle with a little olive oil (particularly at the edges of the naan breads). Bake in the oven for 10–12 minutes until the edges are just golden and the toppings are hot and softened.

Meanwhile, make the raita by mixing the coconut yogurt and mint together in a bowl. Season with salt and set aside.

Remove the naan pizzas from the oven, season with plenty of black pepper and scatter with coriander. Drizzle with the raita, or simply serve it alongside as a dipping sauce.

EASY TIP

Many shop-bought naan breads are suitable for vegans, but always check the ingredients, as they can sometimes contain dairy products. Feel free to use mini naan breads for individual pizzas, if you prefer.

PEAN

BUTT

UT
ER

CREAMY PEANUT SLAW

SERVES 4

2 rounded tbsp smooth
  peanut butter

1 tbsp dark soy sauce

juice of 1 unwaxed lime

pinch of chilli (red pepper) flakes

½ small red cabbage,
  finely shredded

2 large carrots, peeled and thinly
  sliced into matchsticks

1 red (bell) pepper, thinly sliced

1 celery stick, finely chopped

generous handful of coriander
  (cilantro), roughly torn

2 spring onions (scallions),
  chopped

1 tbsp sesame seeds

2 tbsp roasted peanuts

Coleslaw with a twist – crunchy matchstick vegetables with a creamy peanut butter dressing tossed through. Serve with teriyaki burgers with grilled pineapple and chilli mayo (page 205) or load into a jacket potato.

Add the peanut butter to a large bowl and soften slightly with a spoon, then whisk in 100ml (scant ½ cup) boiling water and the soy sauce. Mix until combined and smooth, whisking in a little extra water if needed to make a sauce with the consistency of double (heavy) cream. Whisk in the lime juice and chilli flakes.

Toss in the cabbage, carrots, pepper, celery, coriander, spring onions, sesame seeds and peanuts and stir to evenly coat everything in the peanut sauce.

EASY TIP

This slaw will keep for up to 5 days in the fridge in a sealed container.

SWEET AND SPICY CAULIFLOWER WINGS

SERVES 4

1 cauliflower, broken into large
    florets, leaves discarded

1 tbsp sunflower oil

2 tbsp crunchy peanut butter

2 tbsp BBQ sauce (ensure vegan)

1 tbsp soft light brown sugar

generous pinch of chilli (red
    pepper) flakes

½ tsp sea salt

generous drizzle of hot sauce

small handful of cilantro
    (coriander), roughly torn
    (optional)

unwaxed lime wedges, to serve
    (optional)

Serve these moreish cauliflower 'wings' as a tasty hot snack, or as a side to slow-cooked pulled jackfruit chilli (page 165). The peanut butter is the magic ingredient here, creating a sauce that is thick enough to cling to the cauliflower and becoming stickier and richer as it bakes in the oven. Keep the florets on the larger side, so they stay firmer after roasting.

Preheat the oven to 180°C/350°F/gas mark 4.

Lay the cauliflower florets out on a large roasting tray, or over two smaller roasting trays, leaving some space between them to roast. Drizzle with the sunflower oil, then roast in the oven for 20 minutes.

Meanwhile, add the peanut butter, BBQ sauce, sugar and chilli flakes to a pan with 150ml (generous ½ cup) cold water. Bring to a gentle simmer over a medium heat until combined and smooth, then stir in the salt.

Remove the roasting tray from the oven and carefully dip each floret into the peanut sauce, using tongs or a tablespoon, shaking off any excess sauce. Place back on the roasting tray.

Bake for a further 12–15 minutes until bubbling and light brown at the edges.

Allow to cool for a few minutes, then drizzle with your favourite hot sauce. Scatter with coriander and serve with the lime wedges, if using.

EASY TIP

The edges of the cauliflower crisp up really well in the oven, so there's no need to spend time coating them in breadcrumbs.

FIVE-MINUTE SPICY PEANUT SAUCE

SERVES 4

2 rounded tbsp smooth
   peanut butter

2 tbsp dark soy sauce

pinch of Chinese five-spice

pinch of chilli (red pepper) flakes

2 spring onions (scallions),
   finely chopped

juice of 1 unwaxed lime

This versatile sauce can be used in stir-fries, as a dip, to marinate tofu and vegetables, as a salad dressing – even as a sandwich condiment. It will keep well in the fridge for up to 5 days.

Add the peanut butter, soy sauce, Chinese five-spice and chilli flakes to a pan along with 150ml (generous ½ cup) cold water and warm over a medium-high heat for 3–4 minutes, stirring until combined and glossy.

Stir in the spring onions and lime juice. Serve warm or allow to cool.

EASY TIP

Add more water if you're creating a stir-fry sauce, and less water if you're making a dip.

PEANUT BUTTER BLACK BEAN BURGERS WITH AVOCADO AND APPLE SALSA

SERVES 6

1 x 400g (14oz) can of black beans

1 x 400g (14oz) can of red kidney beans

4 tbsp oats

4 spring onions (scallions), finely chopped

2 rounded tbsp peanut butter

½ tsp mild chilli powder

½ tsp smoked paprika

pinch of ground cinnamon

small handful of coriander (cilantro) leaves, torn

pinch of sea salt and black pepper

2 tbsp sunflower oil, for frying

6 bread buns, halved

1 beef tomato, cut into 6 slices

generous handful of wild rocket (arugula)

For the salsa

1 avocado, diced

1 green apple, diced

5 cherry tomatoes, quartered

generous handful of coriander (cilantro), finely chopped

juice of 1 unwaxed lime

generous pinch of sea salt

Add smooth peanut butter to this burger mix, and you won't look back! Not only does it bring a moreish flavour, but it helps to hold the bean burgers together – because who wants a crumbly burger? Spoon over plenty of avocado and apple salsa for a creamy, juicy zing.

Drain and rinse the black beans and kidney beans and dry on kitchen paper or a clean tea towel. Add both beans to a blender jug or food processor, along with the oats, spring onions, peanut butter, chilli powder, paprika, cinnamon, coriander, salt and pepper. Pulse a few times until a semi-smooth mixture is formed (you may have to scrape the mixture down the sides of the blender) leaving a few chunky beans for texture.

Shape into burger patties using 2 tablespoons of the mixture per burger, or press into a burger shaper to a thickness of 2.5–3cm (1in). Place the 6 burger patties onto a plate and cover with cling film (plastic wrap). Refrigerate overnight, or for at least 6 hours.

Add the oil to a large frying pan over a medium heat, then add the burgers (do this in batches to avoid overcrowding). Cook for 5–6 minutes and then turn to cook the other side for another 5–6 minutes. Keep the burgers warm.

Meanwhile make the salsa. Add all of the ingredients to a bowl and stir to combine.

Warm the bread buns on a griddle (grill) pan for a few seconds, then add a tomato slice to each one. Add a burger, then load in the salsa and top with rocket.

EASY TIP

Allow the burgers to cook for a good 5–6 minutes in the hot pan before flipping, so they stay nice and firm, ready for turning.

CORN ON THE COB PEANUT CURRY

SERVES 2

4 corn on the cob 'cobettes',
   or 2 corn on the cob, halved

1 tbsp sunflower oil

1 onion, finely diced

3 garlic cloves, crushed

3cm (1¼in) piece of ginger, grated

1 tsp garam masala

1 tsp ground turmeric

½ tsp ground cumin

½ tsp chilli (red pepper) flakes

generous pinch of mustard seeds

1 x 400ml (14fl oz) can of full-fat
   coconut milk

2 tbsp tomato purée (paste)

2 rounded tbsp smooth
   peanut butter

1 bay leaf

generous pinch of sea salt

small handful of coriander
   (cilantro), torn

handful of salted peanuts,
   roughly chopped

Combine buttery and nostalgic corn on the cob with a nutty, moreish curry. Spoon the spicy curry sauce over the corn, and get messy eating it with your fingers. Alternatively, you can remove the corn kernels first by standing the cobs on their flat end and using a sharp knife to remove the sweetcorn, before stirring it into the curry. Serve with rice or vegan naan bread and finish with a squeeze of lime, if you like.

Bring a large pan of water to the boil and throw in the cobettes. Simmer for 8 minutes until tender, then drain the water and set aside.

Add the oil, onion, garlic, ginger, garam masala, turmeric, cumin, chilli flakes and mustard seeds to a pan over a low heat and cook gently for 10 minutes, stirring occasionally until the onions have softened but not browned.

Pour in the coconut milk, then stir in the tomato purée and peanut butter. Add a splash of cold water and the bay leaf. Bring to a gentle simmer over a medium-low heat and simmer for 35–40 minutes, stirring frequently, adding a little more cold water if the sauce looks like it's drying out.

Discard the bay leaf, then season the sauce with salt to taste. Add the corn pieces and heat through for 2–3 minutes.

Ladle into bowls and scatter with the coriander and chopped salted peanuts.

EASY TIP

You can find pre-sliced or mini 'cobettes' in supermarkets, or simply use a very sharp knife to cut through each standard-size corn on the cob.

SWEET POTATO PEANUT STEW ❄

SERVES 4

1 tbsp sunflower oil

1 red onion, finely chopped

2 sweet potatoes, peeled and
    sliced into bite-sized cubes

2 garlic cloves, crushed

½ tsp ground cumin

½ tsp ground turmeric

½ tsp chilli (red pepper) flakes

pinch of ground cinnamon

1 x 400g (14oz) can of chopped
    tomatoes

1 tbsp tomato purée (paste)

2 tbsp smooth peanut butter

generous handful of shredded
    kale, tough stems discarded

pinch of sea salt

Every vegan needs a good sweet potato stew recipe in their repertoire, and this version is both simple to make and satisfying to eat. This is my perfect midweek meal, as I usually have all of the ingredients available, plus it's fuss-free to cook. Nothing beats comforting bowl-food.

Add the oil, onion and sweet potatoes to a large pan over a medium-high heat and cook for 4-5 minutes until the sweet potato cubes begin to soften.

Add the garlic, cumin, turmeric, chilli flakes and cinnamon and cook for a further 2 minutes, stirring frequently to prevent catching.

Pour in the chopped tomatoes and tomato purée, then stir in the peanut butter along with a splash of cold water. Bring to a simmer and cook for 25 minutes, stirring frequently.

Add the kale and cook for a further 5 minutes.

Remove from the heat and season to taste with sea salt.

EASY TIP

If you want the stew to stretch a little further, add a can of drained and rinsed red kidney beans. Perfect for packing in the protein!

STICKY MISO AUBERGINE AND SMOKED TOFU

SERVES 4

225g (8oz) block of pre-pressed extra-firm smoked tofu

2 aubergines (eggplants), diced into bite-sized chunks

2 tbsp sunflower oil

3cm (1¼in) piece of ginger, finely grated

2 garlic cloves, crushed

pinch of chilli (red pepper) flakes

1 rounded tbsp white miso

2 rounded tbsp smooth peanut butter

1 tbsp maple syrup

2 tsp sesame seeds

handful of chives, finely chopped

Pack in the flavours here with smoky tofu, tender aubergine and sweet and salty maple-miso-peanut sauce. A tasty midweek meal that is perfect served with steamed rice or Tenderstem broccoli (broccolini).

Preheat the oven to 180°C/350°F/gas mark 4.

Blot the block of tofu on a few sheets of kitchen paper to remove any excess moisture, then cut into bite-sized chunks. Arrange the diced tofu and aubergine pieces over one large roasting tray, or two smaller trays to avoid overcrowding. Drizzle with 1 tablespoon of the sunflower oil, then roast in the oven for 20 minutes.

Meanwhile, add the remaining tablespoon of oil to a pan and throw in the ginger, garlic and chilli flakes. Cook for 2 minutes over a medium heat until fragrant.

Stir in the miso, peanut butter and maple syrup, along with 100ml (scant ½ cup) cold water, and simmer gently until combined, stirring frequently. Set aside.

Remove the roasting tray from the oven and pour the miso peanut sauce over the top, stirring to coat the aubergine and tofu in the sauce. Return to the oven for 5–6 minutes until the sauce is thickened and bubbling.

Remove the roasting tray from the oven and scatter with the sesame seeds and chives just before serving.

EASY TIP

Smoked tofu can be found in most supermarkets and is an easy way to pack a dish with depth of flavour.

PB BREAKFAST SMOOTHIE

SERVES 1

200ml (scant 1 cup) oat milk, chilled

1 tbsp smooth peanut butter

1 banana, peeled

4 strawberries

pinch of grated nutmeg

ice cubes, to serve

Some mornings you need a quick boost of energy and nutrition. This smoothie will see you through until lunchtime, with creamy oat milk, peanut butter and fruit. For a thicker smoothie, use frozen banana; simply freeze your banana in chunks the night before.

Add the oat milk, peanut butter, banana, strawberries and nutmeg to a high-powered blender jug and blitz on high until smooth.

Add the ice cubes to a glass and pour over the smoothie.

EASY TIP

There's no need to remove the leaves of the strawberries, simply blitz to enjoy the whole fruit.

FIVE-INGREDIENT PEANUT BUTTER COOKIES

MAKES 8

100g (3½oz) vegan butter

2 tbsp smooth peanut butter

100g (¾ cup) plain (all-purpose) flour

100g (½ cup) soft light brown sugar

generous pinch of sea salt

If you ever needed proof that the simplest things in life are the best, these cookies will show you how good peanut butter baked goods really are! They spread a little during baking, so make sure you leave some space between each cookie. Throw in a handful of vegan chocolate chips, or some chopped macadamia nuts, if you like. Remember that cookies harden up as they cool, so they will be quite soft when you remove them from the oven, but will cool to the perfect texture.

Preheat the oven to 180°C/350°F/gas mark 4 and line two baking trays with baking parchment.

Heat the butter and peanut butter in a pan over a low heat until melted. Stir to combine and allow to cool for a few minutes.

Add the flour, sugar and sea salt to a bowl and stir together. Pour in the melted butter and peanut butter and stir to combine into a thick dough.

Create 8 small balls from the dough, rolling them in your hands until smooth. Place on the baking tray, making sure you leave plenty of space between each one, and press down. Use a fork to press a criss-cross pattern on the top.

Bake in the oven for 10–12 minutes until the edges are light golden. Once removed from the oven allow to cool for 10 minutes on the tray, then carefully transfer to a wire rack and allow to firm up as they cool.

EASY TIP

For a flavour variation, try switching the peanut butter for cashew nut butter. Sprinkle the cookies with a little icing (confectioner's) sugar to decorate, if you like.

EASY TIP

Switch the strawberry jam for thinly sliced banana, if you like, or try banana jam for a flavour sensation, if you can source it.

DOUBLE PB&J SCONES ❄

MAKES 12

250ml (1 cup) oat milk, plus 1 tbsp
for glazing

2 rounded tbsp crunchy
peanut butter

400g (3 cups) self-raising flour,
plus extra for dusting

½ tsp ground cinnamon

pinch of sea salt

120g (4oz) vegan butter, chilled

2 tbsp caster (superfine) sugar

To serve

strawberry jam

8 strawberries, each cut
into 3 slices

smooth peanut butter

**Crunchy peanut butter is baked into these scones, and
then more is smoothed on when served. A fun twist to the
British classic – perfect for afternoon tea. Best served warm
from the oven, with lashings of smooth peanut butter and
strawberry jam.**

Preheat the oven to 200°C/400°F/gas mark 6 and line 2 baking
trays with baking parchment.

Add the oat milk and peanut butter to a pan and place over
a low heat, mixing until fully combined. Allow to cool for a
few minutes.

In a large bowl, stir together the flour, cinnamon and salt, then
rub in the butter until the mixture resembles breadcrumbs. Stir
in the sugar.

Pour in the warm oat milk and peanut butter mix and use a
wooden spoon to bring it together into a dough.

Place the dough on a lightly floured surface and knead very
gently to cover any large cracks in the dough. Use your hands
to press the dough into an even shape about 2–3cm (1in) thick.

Use a scone cutter to press out 12 scones, bringing together the
leftover dough and re-pressing to the same thickness. Place the
scones onto the lined baking trays, then use a pastry brush to
sweep a little oat milk over the tops.

Bake in the oven for 10–12 minutes until light golden and risen.

Allow to cool until you can handle them comfortably.
Cut a scone in half horizontally and spread on a generous
layer of strawberry jam, then lay on the sliced strawberries.
Smooth the other half generously with peanut butter, then
sandwich together.

TOFU

SCRAMBLED TOFU ON TOAST WITH MUSHROOMS AND TOMATO CHUTNEY

SERVES 4

2 rounded tsp vegan butter

pinch of ground turmeric

8 chestnut (cremini) mushrooms, brushed clean and sliced

generous handful of baby spinach leaves

280g (9oz) block of pre-pressed extra-firm tofu, blotted of excess liquid

2 tbsp vegan double (heavy) cream

handful of chives, finely chopped

generous pinch of sea salt and black pepper

4 thick slices of sourdough bread

2 tbsp tomato chutney

Wake up to this creamy scrambled tofu, gently cooked with vegan butter, chestnut mushrooms and spinach, served on toasted sourdough bread. I like to use extra-firm tofu for this recipe, but if you prefer a softer scramble, experiment with silken tofu.

Melt the vegan butter over a low heat in a frying pan. Stir in the turmeric.

Add the mushrooms and spinach and cook for 3–5 minutes until fragrant.

Meanwhile, use a fork to break up the tofu until it resembles scrambled eggs. Add to the pan and coat in the golden butter, then stir in the double cream.

Cook gently for 10 minutes until the tofu is tender, then season to taste with salt and pepper. Stir in the chives.

Toast the sourdough and generously smooth on the tomato chutney. Spoon over the buttery scrambled tofu, mushrooms and spinach. Serve hot.

EASY TIP

Black salt, or kala namak, is a natural seasoning with an egg-like fragrance. If you have some in the cupboard, add a pinch to the pan, or enjoy the earthy, buttery flavours in this dish as they are.

TOFU BAGELS WITH PICKLED RADISH

SERVES 4

4 radishes, thinly sliced

1 spring onion (scallion), thinly sliced

pinch of chilli (red pepper) flakes

4 tbsp cider vinegar

280g (9oz) block of pre-pressed extra-firm tofu, blotted of excess liquid

1 tbsp sunflower oil

2 rounded tbsp smooth peanut butter

2 tsp light soy sauce

1 tsp sesame seeds

4 bagels, sliced

small handful of coriander (cilantro), roughly torn

drizzle of sriracha sauce

Try this twist on the classic banh mi Vietnamese sandwich for brunch, with lightly toasted, chewy bagels. Choose good-quality, pre-pressed tofu and pan-fry it until golden, then simply allow the pickled radishes, peanut butter and hot sauce to shine!

Add the radishes, spring onion and chilli flakes to a bowl and spoon over the cider vinegar. Allow to stand for at least 1 hour, or overnight, to pickle.

Cut the block of tofu horizontally into 4 slices, then cut each slice into 3 triangles.

Heat the sunflower oil in a flat pan over a medium-high heat, then add the tofu triangles. Cook for 4–5 minutes until crisp and golden, then use tongs to turn the tofu. Cook for another 4 minutes on the other side.

Meanwhile, in a small bowl, mix together the peanut butter, soy sauce and sesame seeds.

Lightly toast the bagels, then spread over the peanut butter mix.

Load the hot tofu into the bagels, then spoon in the pickled radishes. Sprinkle in the coriander and drizzle over the sriracha sauce to taste.

EASY TIP

The radishes and peanut spread can be prepared the night before, for a fuss-free brunch or lunch.

POTATO AND ONION TOFU FRITTATA

SERVES 4

½ tsp vegan butter, for greasing

280g (9oz) block of pre-pressed extra-firm tofu

pinch of ground turmeric

3 tbsp vegan double (heavy) cream

100g (3½oz) hard vegan cheese, grated

1 small onion, diced

5 cooked new potatoes, fully cooled and sliced

generous pinch of sea salt and black pepper

This make-ahead frittata is the perfect addition to any brunch, or is delicious as a simple lunch. Chill after cooking to allow it to set fully, and for the flavours to mingle. Serve chilled or at room temperature, with a green salad or a spoonful of chutney.

Preheat the oven to 200°C/400°F/gas mark 6 and grease a round 18cm (7in) baking tin or pan with vegan butter.

Blot the tofu on kitchen paper to remove any excess liquid, then break up into a few pieces and add to a high-powered blender jug or food processor. Add the turmeric and vegan cream, along with 50ml (scant ½ cup) cold water. Blitz until a thick, smooth paste is formed, scraping the sides of the blender jug as you go. On the final blitz, add another 2–3 tablespoons cold water to loosen the mix, but add gradually as it should remain thick enough to be spooned.

Stir in most of the grated vegan cheese, reserving a handful for later, and season with salt and pepper. Fold in the diced onion and potato slices.

Spoon the mixture into the baking tin or pan, smoothing over the top. Scatter with the remaining cheese.

Bake in the oven for 40–45 minutes until golden and set. Allow to cool fully, then refrigerate overnight or for at least 4 hours until firm. Slice up just before serving.

EASY TIP

If you don't have leftover new potatoes, use canned potatoes. These trusty staples are long-lasting, cheap to buy, and handy to throw into curries and casseroles.

WEEKNIGHT POKE BOWL

SERVES 2

100g (½ cup) sushi rice

generous pinch of smoked sea salt

1 tbsp sunflower oil

1cm (½in) piece of ginger, grated

280g (9oz) block of pre-pressed
extra-firm tofu, blotted of
excess moisture, cut into cubes

1 tbsp dark soy sauce

4 tbsp frozen or fresh
edamame beans

drizzle of sriracha hot sauce
(optional)

½ watermelon, cut into cubes,
seeds discarded

5cm (2in) piece of cucumber,
cut into cubes

1 avocado, cut into cubes

½ red onion, very finely chopped

2 carrots, thinly sliced into ribbons
using a vegetable peeler

juice of ½ unwaxed lime

This simple and fresh poke bowl is the perfect light supper, and a great way to pack in those nutrients. Use a Y-shaped vegetable peeler to make perfect carrot ribbons. I love the addition of juicy watermelon, but mango is a great alternative. Get ahead of the game and prepare the rice, tofu and edamame beans a day in advance, then simply reheat and add them to the bowl.

Place the sushi rice into a sieve and rinse thoroughly with cold water to remove the excess starch. Add the rice to a pan and cover with cold water, then bring to a simmer and cook over a medium heat for 10–12 minutes until plump. Remove from the heat and secure a lid over the pan. Allow to steam for 10 minutes, then fluff it up with a fork and season with the smoked sea salt.

Heat the oil in a frying pan or wok over a medium heat and throw in the ginger and tofu. Cook for 10 minutes, turning the tofu a few times until golden brown. Stir through the soy sauce and cook for a further minute until it is absorbed.

Add the edamame beans to another pan and cover with boiling water from the kettle. Cook for 3–4 minutes until piping hot, then drain.

Spoon the rice, tofu and edamame beans into 2 serving bowls and drizzle the tofu with sriracha hot sauce, if you like.

Divide the watermelon, cucumber, avocado, red onion and carrot ribbons between the 2 bowls, then drizzle over the lime juice to serve.

EASY TIP

If reheating pre-prepared rice, always make sure it is piping hot before serving.

IN-AND-OUT KATSU CURRY WITH GOLDEN TOFU ✳

SERVES 2

For the katsu curry sauce

1 tbsp sunflower oil

1 onion, roughly chopped

1 carrot, peeled and roughly chopped

2cm (¾in) piece of ginger, peeled and roughly chopped

2 garlic cloves, sliced

1 tbsp mild curry powder

1 x 400ml (14fl oz) can of full-fat coconut milk

2 tsp maple syrup

2 tsp soy sauce

1 tsp cornflour (cornstarch)

For the tofu

6 tbsp panko breadcrumbs

1 tbsp sunflower oil

280g (9oz) block of pre-pressed extra-firm tofu, blotted of excess moisture, sliced into fingers

This is one of my favourite ways to eat tofu: crispy, with golden breadcrumbs. Creamy, gently spiced katsu curry is poured over the tofu, but it is also brushed on as a layer beneath the crispy breadcrumbs, for a double hit of flavour.

Start by making the curry sauce. Heat the oil in a large pan over a medium heat and add the onion, carrot and ginger. Cook for 3–4 minutes until the onion begins to soften but not brown.

Add the garlic and curry powder and cook for a further minute, stirring constantly. Pour in the coconut milk, maple syrup and soy sauce.

Mix the cornflour with 1 tablespoon cold water, then stir this into the sauce. Bring to the boil, then simmer for 15 minutes. Allow to cool for a few minutes before pouring the sauce into a high-powered blender jug. Blitz on high until completely smooth, then return to the pan.

Lay out the panko breadcrumbs evenly on a plate. Add the oil to a large frying pan over a low-medium heat.

Brush the tofu fingers with a little of the katsu curry sauce, using a pastry brush or by gently dipping the tofu into the sauce and shaking off any excess, then liberally roll the tofu in the breadcrumbs.

Carefully place the tofu into the hot pan in batches, to avoid overcrowding the pan. Cook the tofu on each side for 2–3 minutes until golden and crisp. Meanwhile, gently reheat the katsu curry sauce over a low-medium heat.

Place the cooked tofu on serving plates, then pour over the extra katsu curry sauce, as liberally as you like.

EASY TIP

Serve with steamed rice or a fresh red cabbage slaw for extra crunch and colour.

SMOKY HERITAGE TOMATO QUICHE

SERVES 4

1 tsp vegan margarine, for greasing

1 sheet of ready-rolled shortcrust pastry (ensure vegan)

1 tbsp sunflower oil

1 onion, diced

2 generous handfuls of spinach leaves

280g (9oz) block of pre-pressed extra-firm smoked tofu

pinch of ground turmeric

3 tbsp vegan double (heavy) cream

100g (3½oz) hard vegan cheese, grated

handful of flat-leaf parsley, finely chopped

2–3 large heritage tomatoes, or 4–5 smaller mixed tomatoes, thickly sliced

sea salt and black pepper

I love a slice of quiche for supper in the summer, with a simple salad or baby new potatoes. This one is a great way to enjoy heritage tomatoes in season. Serve hot or chilled.

Preheat the oven to 180°C/350°F/gas mark 4. Grease an 18cm (7in) loose-bottomed flan tin with vegan margarine or line the base with baking parchment.

Unroll the pastry over the quiche tin, pressing it down into the edges. Trim off the excess pastry.

Line the pastry case with a sheet of baking parchment and add a handful of baking beans (rice or dried pulses also work). Blind bake in the oven for 10 minutes until the pastry becomes lightly golden.

Meanwhile, heat the oil in a pan over a medium heat and add the onion. Cook for 2–3 minutes until it begins to soften, then add the spinach and cook for a further minute. Set aside.

Blot the tofu on kitchen paper or a clean tea towel to remove any excess water, then break up into a few pieces and add to a high-powered blender jug or food processor. Add the turmeric and vegan cream, along with 50ml (scant ½ cup) cold water. Blitz until a thick, smooth paste is formed, scraping the sides of the blender jug as you go. On the final blitz, add up to 2–3 more tablespoons cold water to loosen the mix slightly; it should not be watery but should be thick enough to be spooned.

Stir in the grated cheese and most of the parsley, reserving a pinch for garnishing later, then season with a generous pinch of sea salt and black pepper. Stir in the softened onion and spinach.

Remove the pastry case from the oven and remove the baking beans. Spoon in half of the tofu mix, then lay over half of the sliced tomatoes. Smooth over the remaining tofu mix, and press in the rest of the sliced tomatoes, covering with a very thin layer of tofu mix (to avoid burning).

Bake in the oven for 30–35 minutes until golden and set. Allow to cool for a few minutes before slicing, then sprinkle with the reserved parsley.

EASY TIP

Allow the quiche to cool down for a few minutes before slicing into portions.

EASY TIP

These burgers also cook well on the barbecue, giving an extra
layer of smoky flavour. Cook over direct, medium heat for
3–5 minutes on each side.

TERIYAKI BURGERS WITH GRILLED PINEAPPLE AND CHILLI MAYO

SERVES 2

For the tofu burgers

100ml (scant ½ cup) soy sauce

2 tbsp soft brown sugar

1 tbsp maple syrup

1 tbsp mirin

2 garlic cloves, crushed

2cm (¾in) piece of ginger, peeled and grated

pinch of chilli (red pepper) flakes

280g (9oz) block of pre-pressed extra-firm tofu, blotted of excess liquid

1 tbsp sunflower oil

For the chilli mayo

2 tbsp vegan mayonnaise

6 drops of hot sauce

pinch of sea salt

To finish

2 large bread buns, sliced

drizzle of sunflower oil

2 rings of pineapple (canned or fresh)

½ red onion, thickly sliced

4 leaves of baby gem lettuce

1 tsp sesame seeds

These grilled burgers have a sticky, dark glaze that falls apart into tender, fluffy tofu in the centre. Teriyaki gives the perfect balance of sweet, savoury and heat, which is especially delicious with juicy grilled pineapple and red onions.

Add the soy sauce, brown sugar, maple syrup, mirin, garlic, ginger and chilli flakes to a pan. Place over a medium heat for 5–6 minutes until the mixture is bubbling, then remove from the heat and allow to cool for a few minutes.

Slice the block of tofu horizontally in two, then score the surface of each slice with a sharp knife. Place the tofu slices into a deep dish, then pour over the teriyaki marinade. Allow to stand for at least 1 hour, or overnight if you can, turning the tofu once.

To cook the burgers, brush a griddle (grill) pan with the tablespoon of sunflower oil and place over a medium heat. Lift the tofu out of the marinade and shake off any excess, then place into the pan. Cook for 5–6 minutes on each side until grill lines appear on the tofu. Keep warm.

To make the chilli mayo, stir together the vegan mayonnaise, hot sauce and sea salt. Set aside.

Place the bread buns into a hot griddle pan, cut side down, for a few seconds until grill lines appear. Then place them on serving plates and smooth with a layer of the chilli mayo.

Heat the sunflower oil in the griddle pan over a high heat, then add the pineapple and onion slices. Griddle for 2–3 minutes until hot and sticky.

Add 2 lettuce leaves to each bun, followed by the griddled tofu, pineapple and red onion. Scatter with the sesame seeds and serve hot.

BAKED CORONATION TOFU WITH MANGO

SERVES 2

4 rounded tbsp plain soya yogurt

1 tbsp sunflower oil

2 tsp medium curry paste
  (ensure vegan)

1 tbsp mango chutney

pinch of ground turmeric

pinch of ground cumin

pinch of chilli (red pepper) flakes

pinch of sea salt

280g (9oz) block of pre-pressed
  extra-firm tofu, cut into
  bite-sized chunks

1 mango, peeled and diced into
  bite-sized chunks

pinch of black sesame seeds

small handful of coriander
  (cilantro) leaves, roughly torn

unwaxed lemon wedges, to serve

Marinate tofu in lightly spiced yogurt, then bake with sweet mango for a satisfying supper. Serve with fluffy basmati rice, warmed roti or a simple tomato and red onion salad.

In a large bowl, whisk together the yogurt, oil, curry paste, mango chutney, turmeric, cumin, chilli flakes and sea salt until combined.

Add the tofu chunks and turn to coat in the marinade. Cover the bowl with cling film (plastic wrap) or a lid and allow to marinate for at least 30 minutes.

Preheat the oven to 180°C/350°F/gas mark 4 and line a large baking tray with baking parchment.

Shake off any excess yogurt marinade and place the tofu chunks onto the baking tray, along with the chunks of mango. Bake in the oven for 20–25 minutes until golden.

Remove from the oven and scatter over the black sesame seeds and coriander. Serve with lemon wedges for squeezing over.

EASY TIP

This recipe can also be cooked in an air fryer. Simply lay the marinated tofu and mango (in a single layer) in the tray and cook for 10–15 minutes, shaking the tray halfway through cooking.

CRÈME BRÛLÉE

SERVES 4

250ml (1 cup) vegan double (heavy) cream

100g (½ cup) granulated sugar

3 tsp good-quality vanilla extract

pinch of ground turmeric

2 tbsp cornflour (cornstarch)

300g (10oz) silken tofu

2 generous tbsp soft light brown sugar

This is one of my favourite desserts, and it's surprisingly easy to make. When serving to guests, I make the gently set custard in advance, then grill the brown sugar into a crispy, crackling top just before serving, saving precious time and effort. Silken tofu is an excellent and efficient replacement for eggs in this recipe – I won't tell if you don't.

Pour the cream and granulated sugar into a pan, then stir in the vanilla extract and turmeric. Place over a low heat and stir until the sugar has dissolved.

Mix the cornflour with 4 tablespoons water in a cup, then pour into the pan. Bring to the boil over a high heat for 2 minutes, using a balloon whisk to mix continuously, then reduce the heat to low and simmer for 10 minutes, whisking frequently.

Add the silken tofu to a high-powered blender jug and blitz until completely smooth. Pour into the pan and continue to whisk for 5 minutes until combined, hot and smooth.

Pour the custard into individual ramekins, or one larger dish if you like. Refrigerate for 3–4 hours.

Just before serving, preheat the grill to high and sprinkle the tops generously with the brown sugar. Grill for a few minutes until caramelized and bubbling (alternatively, use a small kitchen blowtorch to melt the brown sugar). Serve while the topping is hot, while the lower part of the custard remains chilled.

EASY TIP

Turmeric gives the classic colour to the custard. A small pinch is all you need, so you won't be able to taste it.

CHOCOLATE CHERRY MOUSSE WITH KIRSCH

SERVES 4

100g (3½oz) good-quality dark (bittersweet) chocolate (ensure vegan), broken into even pieces

300g (10oz) silken tofu

4 tbsp maple syrup

2 tbsp vegan double (heavy) cream

1 x 400g (14oz) can of pitted cherries in syrup

2 tbsp kirsch

Combine the bitter-sweet flavour of cherries with bubbly chocolate mousse in this simple, elegant dessert. I love to use canned cherries for this recipe, as it saves a lot of hard work in pitting and reducing into a compôte – and they are just as delicious.

Bring a pan of water to the boil, then reduce to a simmer. Add the chocolate to a heatproof bowl and place the bowl over the pan, making sure the base of the bowl doesn't touch the water. Stir occasionally until the chocolate has melted into a shiny, smooth liquid. Allow to cool for a few minutes.

Add the tofu to a high-powered blender jug and blitz until completely smooth. Add the maple syrup, vegan cream and melted chocolate, then blitz again until completely combined.

Spoon the cherries into a bowl and stir through the kirsch.

Lay out 4 serving dishes (or one large serving dish) and layer in the chocolate mousse, then a thin layer of the cherries, continuing until the dish is full, and finishing with a layer of cherries.

Refrigerate for at least 4 hours before serving.

EASY TIP

The boozy kick of kirsch is a vibrant, grown-up addition to the dessert, but it is equally as delicious without it.

GRAI

NS

BALSAMIC BULGUR WITH ALMOST-OVER SUMMER FRUITS AND BASIL

SERVES 2 GENEROUSLY

4 tbsp bulgur wheat

2 tbsp good-quality balsamic vinegar

2 very ripe plums, stoned and roughly chopped

1 very ripe peach, stoned and roughly chopped

generous handful of ripe raspberries, halved

generous handful of strawberries, sliced

6 cherry tomatoes, halved

generous handful of small basil leaves

generous pinch of sea salt

When your summer soft fruits are almost over, too ripe and juicy to eat on their own, mix up this simple and delicious salad. This is a great way to enjoy bulgur wheat, lightly dressed in sweet, tangy balsamic vinegar. Soft fruits and balsamic are a match made in heaven!

Put the bulgur wheat into a bowl and pour over enough boiling water to just cover it. Place a lid or cling film (plastic wrap) securely over the top, then allow to stand for 15 minutes.

Fork through the softened bulgur wheat, then drizzle in the balsamic vinegar, stirring to evenly distribute the vinegar through the grains.

Spoon the balsamic bulgur into a large serving bowl, then toss in the plums, peach, raspberries, strawberries and tomatoes, stirring gently into the grains.

Scatter over the basil and season with a little sea salt.

EASY TIP

Adapt the recipe for colder seasons using figs, blackberries and pears, with flat-leaf parsley in place of basil.

MARKET SPICE SOUP WITH PEARL COUSCOUS ❄

SERVES 4 GENEROUSLY

1 tbsp olive oil

1 onion, diced

1 celery stick, diced

1 carrot, thinly sliced into half rounds

1 tsp ground cumin

½ tsp ground turmeric

generous pinch of ground cardamom

pinch of ground cinnamon

500g (2 cups) good-quality passata (sieved tomatoes)

500ml (2 cups) hot vegetable stock

1 x 400g (14oz) jar or can of chickpeas, drained and rinsed

4 tbsp pearl couscous

juice of 1 unwaxed lemon

generous pinch of sea salt and black pepper

small handful of flat-leaf parsley, torn

Fill your kitchen with the warming aromas of Moroccan spice markets, as this soup gently simmers away. I love to add hearty chickpeas and pearl couscous – the larger, toasted sister of fine-grained couscous. Couscous is made from wheat, and although it is more processed than other grains, such as bulgur or quinoa, I've included it in this chapter as you can use it in salads instead of other small grains, or as a gentle thickener in soups.

Add the oil, onion, celery and carrot to a large pan and soften over a low-medium heat for 5 minutes.

Stir in the cumin, turmeric, cardamom and cinnamon and cook for a further minute.

Pour in the passata, vegetable stock and chickpeas, then stir in the pearl couscous.

Bring the soup to the boil over a high heat, then reduce the heat and simmer for 20 minutes.

Remove from the heat and stir in the lemon juice, then season to taste with salt and pepper. Ladle into bowls, then garnish with parsley just before serving.

_____

EASY TIP

Other names for pearl couscous include Israeli couscous, giant couscous or ptitim.

EASY TIP

Many supermarkets sell a mix of long-grain rice and wild rice which is easy to cook at home. If you're combining the rice at home, mix 200g (1 cup) long-grain rice with 100g (½ cup) wild rice for the nuttiest flavour.

WHOLE ROASTED CELERIAC WITH CREAMY MUSHROOM WILD RICE

SERVES 4

1 large celeriac (celery root), about 900g/2lb, scrubbed clean and patted dry

1 tbsp olive oil

2 garlic cloves, smashed

For the creamy mushroom wild rice

300g (1½ cups) long-grain rice and wild rice mix (see easy tip)

2 tbsp pine nuts

1 tbsp olive oil

250g (9oz) chestnut (cremini) mushrooms, brushed clean and roughly sliced

2 garlic cloves, crushed

3 tbsp vegan double (heavy) cream

generous handful of flat-leaf parsley

generous pinch of sea salt and black pepper

Roasting a whole celeriac is a simple and elegant way to cook the root vegetable, leaving it sweet and tender, yet firm enough to carve. I love how the addition of flat-leaf parsley freshens up the creamy mushroom rice, but it is also delicious with a few leaves of fresh thyme, particularly in the winter months. Serve on its own as a simple supper, or as part of a Sunday roast dinner.

Preheat the oven to 180°C/350°F/gas mark 4 and lay out a large sheet of foil.

Rub the celeriac all over with the olive oil, then place into the centre of the foil with the smashed garlic cloves around it. Fold the foil tightly around the celeriac and seal at the top. Roast on the bottom shelf of the oven for 2 hours.

After 2 hours, carefully open the foil from the top and the sides, and roast for a further 25–30 minutes until the skin is golden and the celeriac is tender through the centre.

Meanwhile, add the rice mix to a pan and cover with cold water. Bring to the boil over a high heat, then reduce to a medium heat and simmer for 25–30 minutes until plump. Drain the water and rinse.

Add the pine nuts to a dry frying pan and toast for 3–4 minutes over a medium heat until fragrant and golden brown. Set them aside in a bowl.

Heat the oil in the same frying pan, add the mushrooms and soften for 4–5 minutes over a medium-high heat. Add the garlic and cook for a further minute. Remove from the heat and stir in the cream.

Stir the mushroom mix into the rice, followed by the parsley. Season to taste with salt and plenty of pepper.

Remove the celeriac from the oven and allow to cool for a few minutes before carving into slices.

Spoon the creamy mushroom rice onto warmed plates, followed by a slice or two of roasted celeriac. Scatter over the pine nuts.

POMEGRANATE AND APRICOT TABBOULEH WITH BLACK OLIVES

SERVES 4

50g (½ cup) bulgur wheat

30g (1oz) flat-leaf parsley
(including the stalks),
finely chopped

generous handful of mint leaves,
finely chopped

8 soft dried apricots, diced

8 pitted black olives, sliced
into rounds

seeds from 1 pomegranate,
or 200g (7oz) shop-bought
prepared seeds

juice of 1 large unwaxed lemon

2 tbsp good-quality extra virgin
olive oil

generous pinch of sea salt

This is one of those salads that tastes better after a day, after the flavours have all got to know each other. Sweet, salty, savoury and citrus – it has it all. Serve as a side to date, chickpea and lemon tagine (page 88) or as a tasty lunch.

Place the bulgur wheat in a bowl and pour over enough boiling water to just cover it. Place a plate or cling film (plastic wrap) securely over the top and allow to stand for 15 minutes.

Meanwhile, in a larger bowl, stir together the parsley, mint, apricots, olives and pomegranate seeds.

Fork through the bulgur, then add it to the bowl. Stir to distribute the herbs and fruits, then add the lemon juice.

Stir in the olive oil, then season to taste with salt.

EASY TIP

Bring your unwaxed lemon to room temperature before using, to squeeze the most amount of juice from it.

SPRINGTIME PEARL BARLEY RISOTTO

SERVES 4

1 tbsp olive oil

1 onion, diced

2 garlic cloves, crushed

300g (1½ cups) pearl barley

glug of white wine (ensure vegan)

1 litre (4 cups) hot vegetable stock

generous handful of fresh spring greens, thinly sliced

100g (3½oz) asparagus, roughly chopped, tougher stems discarded

2 tbsp frozen or fresh podded broad (fava) beans

2 tbsp frozen or fresh peas

2 rounded tbsp vegan crème fraîche

juice of ½ unwaxed lemon

generous handful of flat-leaf parsley, finely chopped

small handful of mint leaves, finely chopped

generous pinch of sea salt and black pepper

Make this risotto on those cooler spring days, when you need something warming and comforting but want to celebrate the vibrant produce of the season. Pearl barley is a brilliant alternative to risotto rice, with a nuttier flavour and a plump, al dente texture. This risotto is less 'hands on' than the classic rice-based version, as it doesn't need as much stirring.

Heat the oil in a large pan, add the onion and cook over a low-medium heat for 4–5 minutes until it starts to soften but not brown, then stir in the garlic and cook for a further minute.

Add the pearl barley and stir through the glug of white wine, increasing the heat to medium. Cook for 2 minutes.

Pour in the vegetable stock and bring to a gentle simmer, then cook for 40 minutes, stirring occasionally.

Stir in the spring greens, asparagus, broad beans and peas and cook for a further 10 minutes.

When most of the stock has been absorbed, remove from the heat. Stir in the vegan crème fraîche and lemon juice, then stir through the parsley and mint. Season generously with salt and pepper. Serve hot.

EASY TIP

Switch up the flavours with the seasons – try adding chopped roasted beetroot (beets), walnuts and thyme, or wild mushroom with apple and truffle-infused oil.

PAN-FRIED ARTICHOKES WITH YOGURT AND CRISPY QUINOA

SERVES 4

For the crispy quinoa

100g (½ cup) quinoa

2 tbsp olive oil

pinch of sea salt

For the artichokes

1 x 400g (14oz) can of artichokes, drained and rinsed

1 tbsp olive oil

5 rounded tbsp vegan Greek-style yogurt

handful of chives, finely chopped

small handful of mint leaves, finely chopped

generous pinch of sea salt

Canned artichokes are a great addition to your pantry – perfect for pan-frying, slicing onto a pizza or throwing into a stew. Serve these hot, golden artichokes with herby yogurt and (unexpectedly) crispy quinoa, which has a toasted flavour, reminiscent of salted popcorn, but with crunch.

Add the quinoa to a pan and cover with about 300ml (1½ cups) cold water. Bring to the boil over a high heat, then reduce the heat and simmer for 25 minutes. When the water has been absorbed, remove from the heat and cover the pan with a lid for 5 minutes. Remove the lid and allow the quinoa to cool for 15–20 minutes.

Preheat the oven to 190°C/375°F/gas mark 5 and line a baking tray with baking parchment.

Stir the olive oil and salt into the quinoa, then spread the quinoa out on the baking tray, in as thin a layer as possible. Bake in the oven for 15 minutes, then carefully stir and return to the oven for a further 15–20 minutes until golden and crispy. Remove from the oven and allow to cool for a few minutes.

Meanwhile, blot the artichokes with kitchen paper to remove any excess liquid. Heat the oil in a frying pan over a medium-high heat and add the artichokes. Cook for 15 minutes, turning a few times, until gently browned.

Add the yogurt to a bowl and stir in the chives and mint. Spoon the yogurt mix onto a serving plate, then top with the hot artichokes. Generously scatter over the crispy quinoa and season with a generous pinch of salt.

EASY TIP

Any excess crispy quinoa can be kept in a sealed container for up to 3 days – it makes the perfect alternative to croutons in soups and salads.

SLOW-ROASTED TOMATO, BARLEY AND BEAN STEW ❄

SERVES 4

300g (10oz) cherry tomatoes

1 tbsp olive oil, plus extra
    for drizzling

1 whole bulb of garlic

1 onion, thinly diced

1 large carrot, peeled and chopped
    into half rounds

1 celery stick, diced

1 tsp dried oregano

1 x 400g (14oz) can of good-quality
    chopped tomatoes

600ml (2½ cups) hot
    vegetable stock

4 tbsp pearl barley

1 x 400g (14oz) can or jar of
    cannellini beans, drained
    and rinsed

4 stalks of cavolo nero, roughly
    sliced (tough stems discarded)

generous pinch of sea salt and
    black pepper

handful of small basil leaves

This stew requires patience but is worth the wait, with two-hour roasted tomatoes and garlic stirred into a slowly simmered barley and bean stew. Serve with crusty bread or creamy mashed potatoes.

Preheat the oven to 140°C/280°F/gas mark 1.

Arrange the tomatoes on a baking tray and drizzle with the tablespoon of olive oil. Place the garlic bulb onto a sheet of foil, drizzle with a little olive oil and securely wrap around the garlic. Add to the baking tray next to the tomatoes. Place in the oven to slow-roast for 2 hours until the tomatoes have wrinkled and appear rich in colour, and the garlic has softened.

Meanwhile, add a drizzle of olive oil to a pan and add the onion, carrot and celery. Cook for 5–6 minutes over a medium heat until the onion has started to soften but not brown.

Stir in the oregano, then pour in the canned chopped tomatoes, hot vegetable stock and pearl barley. Bring to the boil, then reduce the heat to low-medium and simmer for 40 minutes, stirring frequently.

Add the beans, cavolo nero and slow-roasted tomatoes. Squeeze in the now-soft garlic cloves, discarding the papery skins, and cook for a further 5 minutes.

Remove from the heat and season to taste with salt and plenty of black pepper. Scatter with basil leaves just before serving.

EASY TIP

The tomatoes and garlic can be roasted up to a day in advance and kept in the fridge until ready to use.

BAKED BIRYANI ❄

SERVES 4

1 tbsp medium curry paste
    (ensure vegan)

1 tsp ground turmeric

½ tsp ground cumin

pinch of chilli (red pepper) flakes

600ml (2½ cups) hot
    vegetable stock

400g (2 cups) basmati rice, rinsed

½ cauliflower, broken into
    small florets

1 small red onion, roughly sliced

8 green beans, halved

1 red (bell) pepper, roughly sliced

2 tbsp flaked (slivered) almonds

1 tbsp sultanas (golden raisins)

juice of ½ unwaxed lemon

handful of coriander (cilantro), torn

pinch of sea salt

If you love a 'throw it in the oven' supper as much as I do, then you'll love this spicy biryani, which can be made with any vegetables you have left in the fridge. The combination of cauliflower, red onion, green beans and peppers is my favourite, but you could also use carrots, sweetcorn, sweet potato, butternut squash or peas.

Preheat the oven to 200°C/400°F/gas mark 6.

Add the curry paste, turmeric, cumin and chilli flakes to a jug (pitcher) of the hot vegetable stock and set aside.

Add the rice, cauliflower, red onion, green beans and red pepper to a large, deep roasting tray and scatter over the almonds and sultanas.

Pour the spiced stock mixture into the tray, covering the rice and vegetables fully and stirring to distribute evenly.

Loosely cover the roasting tray with foil, then bake in the oven for 50–55 minutes until the rice is fluffy and the stock has been absorbed.

Remove from the oven and drizzle over the lemon juice. Scatter with coriander and salt before serving.

EASY TIP

If you're planning to eat the leftovers the following day, ensure that the rice is fully cooled before refrigerating. To serve, reheat thoroughly or enjoy cold from the fridge as a spiced rice salad.

FENNEL, CHILLI AND QUINOA ❄

SERVES 4

1 tbsp olive oil

1 onion, diced

1 fennel bulb, thinly sliced

2 garlic cloves, crushed

1 tsp good-quality harissa paste

2 x 400g (14oz) cans of good-
    quality chopped tomatoes

2 tbsp quinoa

1 x 400g (14oz) can or jar of
    butterbeans (lima beans),
    drained and rinsed

generous pinch of sea salt

handful of fresh chives,
    finely chopped

generous handful of flat-leaf
    parsley, finely chopped

fennel fronds, roughly chopped
    (optional)

This is one of my favourite ways to eat quinoa, as the grain thickens the sauce to make a full-flavoured stew. Fennel delivers plenty of sweetness to counteract the acidity of the tomatoes too. Delicious for lunch or supper.

Heat the oil in a pan, add the onion and fennel and soften over a medium heat for 5 minutes. Add the garlic and harissa and cook for a further minute.

Pour in the chopped tomatoes along with 200ml (generous ½ cup) cold water, then add the quinoa and butterbeans. Bring to the boil, then reduce the heat and simmer for 30 minutes, stirring frequently.

When the quinoa is plump, remove from the heat and season to taste with salt. Scatter over the chives, parsley and fennel fronds (if using) just before serving.

EASY TIP

Use a good-quality harissa paste with a balance of flavours. My favourite is Tunisian Berber harissa, which is strong and smoky.

RUM AND RAISIN RICE PUDDING

SERVES 4

150g (½ cup) pudding rice

1 x 400ml (14fl oz) can of full-fat coconut milk

300ml (1½ cups) oat milk

1 tsp vanilla extract

3 tbsp soft light brown sugar

1 tsp grated nutmeg

100ml (scant ½ cup) dark rum (ensure vegan)

4 tbsp muscovado sugar

2 tbsp raisins

Pure comfort food. Short-grain pudding rice cooks down to be soft, creamy and nostalgic; this has the classic flavours of vanilla and brown sugar, but with boozy rum and raisins for added luxury. Coconut milk gives the rice pudding creaminess and works perfectly with the tropical taste of rum.

Add the rice, coconut milk, oat milk, vanilla extract, light brown sugar and nutmeg to a large pan. Bring to the boil, then reduce the heat to a simmer and cook for 25 minutes until the rice has softened and most of the liquid has been absorbed.

Meanwhile, add the rum, muscovado sugar and raisins to a smaller pan and cook over a medium-high heat for 5 minutes until the sugar has dissolved.

Stir most of the rum syrup into the rice pudding, reserving some for topping once ladled into bowls.

EASY TIP

The combination of whisky and candied orange peel makes a great alternative to rum and raisin.

INDEX

ABOUT THE AUTHOR

Katy Beskow is an award-winning cook, writer and cookery tutor with a passion for seasonal ingredients, vibrant food and fuss-free home cooking. Once inspired by a bustling and colourful fruit market in South London, Katy now lives in rural Yorkshire and cooks from a small (yet perfectly functioning) kitchen. She blogs at www.katybeskow.com. Katy is a member of the Guild of Food Writers and is the author of *15-Minute Vegan* (2017), *15-Minute Vegan Comfort Food* (2018), *15-Minute Vegan on a Budget* (2019), *Five Ingredient Vegan* (2019), *Vegan Fakeaway* (2020), *Easy Vegan Bible* (2020), *Vegan Roasting Pan* (2021), *Vegan BBQ* (2022), *Easy Speedy Vegan* (2022), *Easy Vegan Christmas* (2023) and *Thrifty Vegan* (2023); this is her twelfth book.

ACKNOWLEDGEMENTS

Huge thank you to the editorial team at Quadrille. Thank you to Publishing Director Sarah Lavelle for all of the opportunities spanning over twelve books. Heartfelt thanks to Commissioning Editor Stacey Cleworth for your attention to detail and passion for the project; I'm looking forward to working with you again. Special thanks to Harriet Webster for commissioning and believing in the book. Thank you to Copy Editor Clare Sayer and Editorial Assistant Ellie Spence for the excellent editorial support. It is a privilege, as always, to work with you all.

Thank you to Designers Katy Everett and Emily Lapworth for the art direction and design. It really is a beautiful book.

Massive thanks to Photographer Luke Albert, Food Stylist Tamara Vos, Assistant Food Stylists Georgia Rudd and Emma Cantlay and Prop Stylist Louie Waller, for the dedication, knowledge and creativity. Shoot days are always a highlight of the project!

Thank you to Publicity Manager Rebecca Smedley for your ongoing hard work with all of the book campaigns. A big thanks to Marketing Executive Rebecca Knight for your expertise throughout the process. I love working with you both!

Huge thanks, as always, to my wonderful literary agent, Victoria Hobbs, and the team at A.M. Health. I am so grateful for your support, guidance and friendship. Thank you for believing in me since 2016!

To my ever-supportive family: Mum, Dad, Carolyne and Mark. Thank you for your encouragement and kindness, I hope you enjoy this book. Thank you to my beautiful twin nieces, Tamzin and Tara, who fill me with joy and pride. Thank you to Auntie May for your kind words and support throughout the process. Thank you to Pandi, the house rabbit, for your companionship and cuddles.

The biggest thank you goes to you, lovely reader. I hope *Vegan Pantry* becomes a staple cookbook in your kitchen, inspiring you to make the most of store-cupboard essentials and create delicious, nourishing vegan meals.

Managing Director
Sarah Lavelle

Commissioning Editors
Harriet Webster and
Stacey Cleworth

Editorial Assistant
Ellie Spence

Copy Editor
Clare Sayer

Deputy Design Manager
Emily Lapworth

Designer
Katy Everett

Photographer
Luke Albert

Food Stylist
Tamara Vos

Food Stylist Assistants
Emma Cantlay and
Georgia Rudd

Prop Stylist
Louie Waller

Head of Production
Stephen Lang

**Senior Production
Controller**
Sabeena Atchia

First published in 2024 by Quadrille
Publishing Limited

Quadrille
52–54 Southwark Street
London SE1 1UN
quadrille.com

Text © Katy Beskow 2024
Photography © Luke Albert 2024
Design and layout © Quadrille
Publishing Limited 2024

Cataloguing in Publication Data:
a catalogue record for this book is
available from the British Library.

ISBN: 978 1 78713 947 3

Printed in China